FINALLY . . . A PERSONAL FINANCE GUIDE YOU DON'T NEED AN M.B.A. TO UNDERSTAND!

Financially Fearless by 40 walks you through the big issues and dilemmas facing people in their thirties. Whether you want to find the perfect mortgage, open a money market fund, or lower your tax bill by saving for retirement, Jason Anthony answers the questions you've always had but didn't know who to ask.

Praise for Jason Anthony's *Debt-Free by 30*

"*Debt-Free by 30* manages to preach financial fitness to twenty-somethings in a way that gets through the financial haze surrounding a twenty-eight-year-old's head . . . Cluck and Anthony offer sensible first-step approaches to saving money, and more importantly, refraining from spending all of it . . . Practical, positive, and painless, *Debt-Free by 30* is the GenX guide to freedom from limping toward the big 3-0 one minimum payment at a time."

—*BookPage*

Jason Anthony is a film and television executive who has worked in the East Coast offices of some of the biggest producers and directors in Hollywood. He is currently the senior vice president of creative affairs for Laura Ziskin Productions (*Spider-Man* and *Pretty Woman*). The coauthor of *Debt-Free by 30*, he lives in New York.

Also by Jason Anthony

Debt-Free by 30

financially fearless by 40

PRACTICAL ADVICE FOR THE SMART, SUCCESSFUL, AND FINANCIALLY CLUELESS

JASON ANTHONY

A PLUME BOOK

PLUME
Published by the Penguin Group
Penguin Group (USA) Inc., 375 Hudson Street, New York, New York 10014, U.S.A.
Penguin Books Ltd, 80 Strand, London WC2R 0RL, England
Penguin Books Australia Ltd, 250 Camberwell Road,
Camberwell, Victoria 3124, Australia
Penguin Books Canada Ltd, 10 Alcorn Avenue, Toronto, Ontario, Canada M4V 3B2
Penguin Books (N.Z.) Ltd, Cnr Rosedale and Airborne Roads,
Albany, Auckland 1310, New Zealand

Penguin Books Ltd, Registered Offices: 80 Strand, London WC2R 0RL, England

First published by Plume, a member of Penguin Group (USA) Inc.

First Printing, July 2003
1 3 5 7 9 10 8 6 4 2

LIBRARY OF CONGRESS CATALOGING-IN-PUBLICATION DATA
Anthony, Jason.
Financially fearless by 40 : practical advice for the smart, successful, and financially clueless / Jason Anthony.
p. cm.
Includes index.
ISBN 0-452-28433-3 (pbk.)
1. Finance, Personal. 2. Debt. 3. Professional employees—Finance, Personal. I. Title.

HG179.A568 2003
332.024—dc21
2003048629

Printed in the United States of America
Set in Times New Roman

PUBLISHER'S NOTE
This publication is designed to provide accurate and authoritative information in regard to the subject matter covered. It is sold with the understanding that the publisher is not engaged in rendering legal, accounting or other professional services. If you require legal advice or other expert assistance, you should seek the services of a competent professional.

For my father

ACKNOWLEDGMENTS

Where to start?

First, to my talented editor Kelly Notaras, for adopting me and treating me as one of her own. I can't imagine a better publishing experience. Her enthusiasm, encouragement, and collaborative spirit made my deadline seem almost humane. Without Kelly, I wouldn't be the confident, disciplined, and sleep-deprived writer that I am today.

To Tanya McKinnon, my gifted agent, tireless advocate, and supremely valued friend. Tanya is living proof that business and pleasure really do go together.

To Trena Keating for her patience.

To my team of experts: Rachel Schwarz at Smith Barney, Keith Furer at Apple Mortgage Corp., and Dominic Marsicovetere, C.P.A. I hope the rib eye made it all worth it.

To Elaine Chen, for her technological wizardry and mastery of all things Excel.

To Sarah Melwyk, for getting the word out.

To Google, for saving me from countless Saturdays at the library.

To Amanda Patten, for getting the ball rolling and becoming a friend.

To Richard Simon, Rob McQuilkin, Bill Eville, and Stephen Shapiro for tweaking draft after draft after draft.

To Laura Ziskin, for giving me the latitude and encouragement to finish this before the sequel.

To Will Speck, Elyse Kroll, Brian Jones, Alison Appel, and Mary Jean Babic—treasured members of the Special People Club.

And finally, my deepest gratitude to all of those who took the time to share their most personal stories with me. I know it wasn't easy. Your trust, honesty, and insights helped make this a far better book.

CONTENTS

INTRODUCTION

This may hurt a little.

Next time you're alone—you probably don't want anyone around for this—grab a pen and some lined paper. Beginning with the current year and counting backwards, list all the years since your first full-time job. In the next row, list your income for that year. Don't remember? I don't believe you. Salaries are like SAT scores—they become permanently embedded in your gray matter. (If you can legitimately claim amnesia, look up your old tax returns.) Now add up the numbers and write the total at the bottom of the page. Give or take a few years, your worksheet should resemble something like the one on page xii. Now take a good long look at the number on the bottom of your page.

How much of that do you still have?

More importantly, do you have any idea where it all went?

Oh, I know. Taxes take a bite, and yes, everyone has to eat. But even after lopping off fixed expenses, say, 35 percent for taxes, 20 percent for rent, and another 10 percent for food and miscellaneous, the number staring back at you is probably quite a bit more than the $83 on your ATM receipt. Welcome to

Year	Income	Age
1989	$22,000	22
1990	24,675	23
1991	28,500	24
1992	32,746	25
1993	40,241	26
1994	45,000	27
1995	47,610	28
1996	55,000	29
1997	63,415	30
1998	70,352	31
1999	75,405	32
2000	78,210	33
2001	90,000	34
2002	97,300	35
2003	?	36
	$770,454	

your thirties, class. Lesson One: Making more money does not solve your problems. Lesson Two: Getting over your fears and educating yourself will.

How is it that we can go to school, possibly attain a professional degree, build a successful career, and yet manage to avoid Personal Finance 101? It seems to me that the time to learn this stuff is *before* we enter the real world, while our minds are still young and impressionable. As anyone who's tried to learn a foreign language as an adult knows, it's *mas dificil* to absorb this stuff later in life. Perhaps some people resent learning new things after a certain age, or maybe they assume if they don't understand it by now, they never will. Or maybe our brains just get full.

Whatever the reason, financial ignorance has very real consequences. Here's one example: After graduating from high school, my lovely stepsister lived at home for a while. One day my father asked her how she was doing with her savings. "Fine," she replied. "How much do you have in the bank?" my father asked. "I don't know," she said. "Then how do you know you're doing fine?" my father asked. "Because I still have a lot of checks left," she answered.

That night my father took control of her bank account.

My stepsister was 18 at the time (she's a lot smarter now as a 33-year-old mother of two), but still I've met people in their thirties who are almost as oblivious as my stepsister was at 18. Unfortunately, the ramifications to their financial well-being go far beyond a few bounced checks. For example, I spoke to one 33-year-old guy who bartends once in a while and gets paid in cash. So far he's saved over $5,000 from the gigs, yet he won't invest it for fear that the IRS will notice he has too much money on hand. (They won't.) Instead, he keeps the $5,000 stuffed in a bag in his freezer! Now, if he were to stash that $5,000 into an investment account with a 7 percent return instead of giving his Andrew Jacksons a mean case of frostbite, this is how much he would have upon retirement:

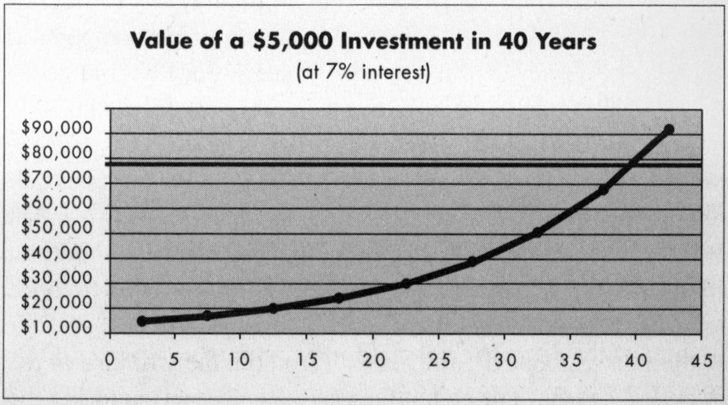

The Road to Fearlessness

Forget what they told you about your twenties. This is the decade that really matters. Think about all the milestones many of us hit in our thirties—we get hitched, we have kids, we have savings for the first time ever, and we scrimp for our little quarter-acre of Heaven. We change jobs, we change careers—hell, some of us even change our sexual preference. On the personal Geiger counter, these decisions are nothing short of seismic. Yet many of us continue to stumble through our fourth decade, afraid or unwilling to lay the foundation of the rest of our lives.

My first book, *Debt-Free by 30,* was a kind of personal finance version of MTV. It was written for people in their twenties who only thought about money when they didn't have any. You can think of this book as the next step—a financial VH-1. *Debt-Free* understood the trauma of being a twentysomething buried in debt and showed how to get out of it. The book you're holding now represents the next step in the financial evolution for all formerly clueless thirtysomethings.

I'm always mystified by the number of personal finance books out there aimed at people in their twenties and thirties. Claiming that such one-size-fits-all advice works for everyone frankly strikes me as more than a little out-of-touch. The 23-year-old slacker crashing on his friend's couch probably shares little in common with a 36-year-old woman staring at her computer at 2 A.M. trying to figure out how she's going to fund her kid's education. If you've ever dated someone in his twenties, you know—usually not a good idea. You want to talk about your regrets, your options, your evolving sense of self, etc. He wants to talk about Matchbox 20 and get down your pants. How likely is it that you and this person speak the same financial language? Youthful innocence has its charms, but can be very hard to relate to once your life has moved on.

Many of us hope the thirties will iron out the wrinkles of the twenties, but that's often not the case. As we start exploring the brave new world of marriages, mortgages, kids, etc., our financial needs change and become increasingly complicated. Callie, a friend of mine in her late thirties, put it like this: "I never thought much about money in my twenties. My priority were clothes, vacations—you know, all the shallow stuff. I thought when I got married the money thing would take care of itself. That whole thing about 'two living as cheaply as one.' Well, now that I'm married money seems to be a bigger issue than ever. My husband and I both do well, but we find ourselves making choices and doing without in ways that I never had to before I had a family. I'm not as frivolous with money anymore, but it doesn't seem to matter. Between our 401(k) plan, the mortgage, our son's education fund, and car insurance, there's very little left over. But those crumbs have caused some huge blow-ups between my husband and me."

Callie married Justin when they were in their thirties. It was the first marriage for both. Even with all the supposed life experience between them, the two often lose perspective when the situation involves money. Callie recalls one particularly painful, but unfortunately common, episode: "I was standing in a furniture store, looking at a great rug on sale. It was $1,500—expensive, yes, but still 70 percent off. I called him on the cell to discuss it, and he just blew up and turned it into a referendum on my abilities as a mother. He asked how I could be so selfish when we needed the money for Brian's education. I thought we were saving enough for school. I left the store in tears."

Without the benefit of financially savvy parents or access to skilled financial advisers, it's easy to feel as if we've been dumped in a strange wilderness without a map. Conversation after conversation, I heard thirtysomethings wrestle with questions like these:

- How does anyone scrape together the money for a down payment on a house?

- How am I ever going to come up with $120,000 for my child's college education?
- My spouse and I have very different definitions of "the good life." How can we compromise before we kill each other?
- Everyone says Social Security is a joke. Why am I not laughing?

Sound familiar?

Besides sharing common concerns, the people I spoke to all seemed to intuitively grasp something else: the stakes are much, much higher in our thirties. It's one thing to squander your paycheck when you're 22 and earning $23,000 a year; quite another when you're pulling in $90,000 and planning to get married and have a kid within the next two years. Many of us enter our prime earning years in our thirties and don't want to waste them being passive. You've probably sat at the Thanksgiving table and had to endure some uncle philosophize about how having money frees you from thinking about it. Bull. Having money frees you from living in a 350-square-foot studio and taking Greyhound home for Christmas. Stop thinking about money, and soon you will have no money to think about.

Money is important—just ask someone who doesn't have any. Money sparks opportunity. It provides shelter from life's hardballs. And, let's be honest, it impresses the hell out of many, many people. For better or for worse, it's the single biggest yardstick Americans use to rank themselves on the social food chain.

Unfortunately, it takes many of us far too long to come around to this realization. After the salad days of our twenties, many of us enter our thirties on a seriously empty stomach. With maturity comes the realization that you don't have to rule the world to be happy. You don't have to star in your own sitcom or serve on the Supreme Court to be happy. A house and a little nest egg will do just fine, thank you. That's the good news. The bad news is, you maybe starting to think that even a house and nest egg will be a pipe dream forever. I'm here to tell you that they won't, and with a little discipline and commitment, you can get them and more.

Who This Book Is for and What You'll Get Out of It

Consider this book the personal finance version of an all-nighter—caffeine for the economically challenged. If you spent your twenties living hand-to-mouth and are in no particular rush to revisit those days, then following the advice in this book will show you the way to a calmer, more rewarding future. Or perhaps you were always practical with your cash, but you want more control of your financial destiny. This book can help. Money, and our relationship to it, grows more complicated as we get older. It's time to let go of the excuses and take responsibility.

I wrote this book for the people out there who'd rather do a hundred other things before picking up a personal finance book. In other words, 99 percent of the thirtysomething population. Let's face it—this stuff can be intimidating. And, yes, even a little boring. (I'll try to keep those parts to a minimum.) Fortunately, however, some kind of biological panic button goes off around the big 3–0, and we realize that it's time to finally get our financial houses in order. Learning this stuff now can pay dividends (which you'll learn all about in Chapter Six) for decades to come.

You'll notice that Chapters One and Two of this book won't teach you much about decoding the business pages or show you how to get in on the next big I.P.O. These chapters focus instead on the emotional life of money, and, believe me, they are every bit as important as identifying the next Microsoft. Over the course of this book I've learned that, as much as anything else, our feelings toward money ultimately determine how much of it we end up with. Being in touch with these feelings is the first step toward establishing a rewarding financial plan and avoiding the monetary sins of the past.

Which is not to downplay the nuts and bolts of money management. Those skills are vital too, and we'll cover them. Chapters Four and Five will show you what you need to do to kiss your landlord good-bye and get the keys to the kingdom. Six and Seven teach you the ins and outs (as well as the ups and downs) of the stock market. Chapter Eight explores the world of mutual funds, an attractive way for novice investors to jump on the equity bandwagon. And because pension plans went out with Peter Frampton, we look at retirement savings vehicles in Chapter Nine. Finally, I'm a realist. I know that many people enter their thirties in negative territory. Chapter Ten offers shortcuts to vanquishing debt for good.

So, you screwed up your twenties. Big deal. The important thing is, you've got your priorities straight now. If you start right away, time is still on your side. Maybe not for your hairline and that paunch your girlfriend swears is "cute," but for a fearless financial future, you're right on time.

financially fearless by 40

1

Emotional Rescue

If you believe that you learn something new every day, it seems that we should all be pretty damn smart by the time we enter our thirties. But sometimes it seems that the older we get, the less we know. Sure, we can now concede that *St. Elmo's Fire* wasn't the pinnacle of '80s cinema we once thought and all those Ayn Rand novels we used to quote from are actually kind of dopey. Those are matters of intellect. They can be researched, debated, proven. But decoding your inner life turns out to be considerably more challenging than watching Judd Nelson emote. (Okay, maybe that's not the best example, but you see my point.)

Many people who aren't reaching their economic potential believe that money and emotions share little connection to each other. They believe that bad luck or lack of financial finesse is holding them back. If they just bone up on the business pages and catch a lucky break, they'll be all right. Sometimes, this is true. More often, however, these people fail to see the real problem. They don't understand how mind and money intersect. Left unresolved, psychological baggage will control your adult life, and all the finance tutorials in the world won't help you if your feelings toward money remain unresolved.

The stakes grow so much higher in our thirties. The money's often bigger, retirement moves a little closer on the horizon, and frankly, most of us just want more stuff. Unfortunately, nobody rids himself of bad habits without first committing to change. When we turn 30, destructive financial habits and patterns don't magically disappear like a Marc Jacobs sweater in Winona's fitting room. They stay with us until we decide we want to conquer them. And for that to happen, we must first discover where we went wrong.

While talking to people for this book I heard one common refrain—all seemed to want greater control over their financial future. Few knew how to make it happen. But almost without exception I discovered that they *did* have the resources to improve their situation. It wasn't going to happen after one coffee together, but in these conversations I found that people had far more control over their financial lives than they thought. On a subconscious level, many people must know this. After all, even the most complacent thirtysomething would have a tough time blaming his financial woes on a $150 student loan payment when he's making $100,000 a year. Yet change is hard, and it's not enough to understand where the problem lies. Self-awareness is only the fuel that drives action. Commitment is the engine.

In this chapter, I've compiled some of the most common emotional pitfalls that befall thirtysomethings. As you read, you will see that there is nothing extraordinary about the people in these stories. All are otherwise intelligent people who nevertheless couldn't get a grip on their financial lives. Many conquered their fears. Others have taken steps to improve. One has not. Regardless of where you fall on the spectrum, I'm betting you'll see a bit of yourself in these pages.

Home Alone

On paper, Jenna looks like a formidable turbo-achiever. She graduated from an Ivy League university and holds a degree from a top law school. Later, she rode the Internet boom to a posh consulting job. When the boom went bust, she segued effortlessly into a senior position in advertising, and today supplements her already ample income writing freelance articles for trade publications. In short, Jenna possesses adaptive skills most of us would kill for. Under the calm surface, however, lurks a truth considerably more tumultuous. At 34, Jenna has only recently pulled the plug on a brutal tug-of-war game with her parents over money.

"The battle really began in my undergraduate years," Jenna explains. "My parents are unapologetic pragmatists. You don't get an education to expand your horizons. You go to college to get a high-paying job. So my early interest in art history, architecture, etc. was pretty much stamped out by my parents. They even gave me an ultimatum—they said if I didn't go preprofessional then they wouldn't pay private school tuition. I would have to transfer to a state school close to home. They also indoctrinated me with their first-generation immigrant fears. You know—'If you don't work 20 hours a day, you'll go broke and starve.' You can imagine the head trip this has on a 17-year-old girl caught between trying to please her parents and figuring things out for herself."

Jenna ultimately did obey her parents and applied to law school, but not without accumulating a huge amount of resentment. That resentment had to find an outlet somewhere. For Jenna it manifested itself in afternoons trawling outlet malls and late-night clubbing when she should have been studying for class. Naturally, her grades tanked. But Jenna says her behavior was more complicated than mere rebellion. "Yes, on one hand I was acting out," she says. "But I was also subconsciously burying myself in debt so I would be in a position where a high-paying law job would be my only way I could pull myself out of it." For Jenna, engaging in such harmful behavior hurt less than accepting that her parents were shoving her down a career she had no interest in pursuing.

Besides the law school loans and the credit card debt, Jenna would intentionally borrow too little money to cover her living expenses. Rationally, she knew she could never survive as a student living in New York City. To get by, she would take out high-interest cash advances on her credit cards, resulting in dire financial straits. Although her behavior boxed Jenna into a corner, it also dulled the anger she felt toward her parents for not letting her lead her own life. Now only a job at a white-shoe law firm could rescue her financially. It was painful for Jenna to acknowledge that her parents didn't trust her to make the right decisions for herself. In effect, she created her own desperate situation to justify her parents' bullying. If her only out was a law job, maybe her parents really did know best.

Not until her early thirties did Jenna establish a healthy equilibrium with her parents. Most of us experience profound, and for the most part positive, changes in our relationship with our parents when we reach adulthood. In their desperation to remain active participants in her adult life, Jenna's parents ruthlessly wielded the money card to keep her bound to them. "My parents use money to reward and punish. During times when they weren't proud of me, they would cut me off without a dime. Of course, these were the times I was in deepest trouble and truly needed the help. When I lost my law job in the recession I owed $80,000 in student loans. I had a panic attack just buying a newspaper and a 75-cent coffee. But all I got from my mother was a lecture. I was staring bankruptcy in the face and all she could say was, 'I knew you weren't working hard enough at that job.' "

After a few years in the professional wilderness, Jenna jumped on the Internet bandwagon, quickly climbing to a six-figure salary and a nice options package. And there were Jenna's parents once again, first waving a blank check for her law school loans and later helping her with a down payment for her house. "Now that they approved of the course my life was taking, they were financially supportive. Even though I didn't need them anymore. I was doing just fine by myself." I ask Jenna if she thinks her parents' generosity was motivated in part by guilt for pushing her toward law school. "Nope," she says. "That's not a word in their vocabulary. It's how they show approval. And I'm not ungrateful for the help. I would still be paying those loans if they hadn't jumped in. But let's call it what it is—an instrument of control."

With a good job, a mortgage, and no debt, Jenna had the opportunity to act like an adult for the first time in her life. She recognized that parental money, whether being withheld or offered, muddied family relationships and profoundly affected her self-image. So determined was she to sever the financial ties that bind, that when her father recently offered her $10,000 to redo her kitchen, Jenna said thanks, but no thanks. "My kitchen desperately needs to be redone, and I certainly don't have that kind of money lying around, but I'll do it when I've saved the money. I'd rather live with ugly Formica than marble countertops that I earned by being a good [read: obedient] daughter."

Jenna's story is a classic example of how discord between parents and adult children can sabotage our economic well-being. Jenna's parents sent her the horrible message that money is more important than happiness, which brought her own belief system into sharp conflict with her parents. Although a fully capable adult, Jenna could never let go of the fears that her parents instilled in her as a child. For far too long she believed that financial control is an acceptable way for a parent to express love. Jenna's parents meant well, but they did their daughter no favors by preventing her from exploring her own dreams and finding her own sources of fulfillment. Caught between trying to be the responsible daughter and the arbiter of her own goals, Jenna was neither.

Love at the Mall

To look at the frugal, responsible, successful 35-year-old Kim now, you would never believe the spendthrift ways she left behind. These days she dresses stylishly but affordably ("No item over $80," she says), and spends most evenings with her husband watching a DVD over a home-prepared meal. That's a far cry from her days as a broke graduate student in Boston struggling with student loans, no income, $7,000 in credit card debt, and one serious compulsive spending problem.

"Here I am in one of the top programs in the country, surrounded by serious brain power, and I'm obsessed with these shoes I saw on sale at Newbury Street. No wonder I felt like a freak up there. People in grad school just don't act that way. I thought I would feel at home in a program surrounded by people with similar interests, but I didn't. I still felt different from other people at school, and not quite as good as everybody else."

Kim represents the classic case of the victim of low self-esteem who tries desperately to compensate through spending. What makes Kim's case interesting, however, is how she used shopping to deflect a multi-pronged assault on her self-esteem. First, she grew up biracial in a homogeneous East Coast suburb ("Before all those Benetton ads made people like me chic," she jokes). While her town wasn't staunchly conservative, her racial makeup did add another dimension to the already difficult adolescent challenge of fitting in. "Teenagers are far more sophisticated and enlightened now," says Kim, "but back then, I was almost a curiosity, with neither side not quite knowing what to make of me. No one else in my little adolescent world shared the experience of growing up biracial. So even if I didn't feel overt prejudice, it could be very lonely at times."

Many people in Kim's situation might ordinarily seek refuge and acceptance at home. For Kim, this was not an option. Her father, who as a young farmer had almost starved during the Depression, had little time for Kim's teenage problems. Worse, he was both physically and verbally abusive to her, and undercut almost everything she did. "I remember one time my mother and father were in the living room fighting about something stupid. I was sitting on the couch watching television. Finally, I couldn't take it anymore and I told my father to leave my mother alone. He looked at me like he could kill me. He walked over to me, grabbed me by the neck, and pulled me off the couch. I screamed and started struggling. He called me a 'stupid little bitch' and punched me so hard I fell on the floor. I was 12 years old."

Kim's mother, more interested in restoring peace than justice, did something that to this day still upsets Kim: she blamed her daughter for provoking her father. "That was the way it always went. She would blame me for any family upheavals because she was terrified of my father. I was the easier target. She couldn't control my father, but she could control me. But afterward she would always feel terribly guilty about it. So she would take me shopping and buy me something."

In time, shopping and love became synonymous in Kim's mind. Her mother couldn't provide the emotional support to help her daughter, so she expressed her love through material possessions. "Her family lost everything in Europe after the War, so, for her, providing material comfort really was the ultimate gesture of love. She meant well, but it laid the foundation for my compulsive spending later on. It's like the parent who offers food to a kid every time she's upset and then the kid grows up to be a chronic overeater. We just went to a store instead of the refrigerator."

Kim started therapy in her late twenties and after three years with a skilled therapist was able to see how shopping was compensating for the self-love and respect she couldn't feel. She credits this recognition—coupled with her fear of a broke future—for her phenomenal self-discipline. She contacted a credit counseling service, which negotiated a better repayment schedule on her behalf and helped her set up a budget she could live with. And she stuck to it.

Over time, the new habits became second nature, and today Kim reports that she is firmly in control of every dollar. Each Sunday night she takes out $200 from the ATM and doesn't return until the following Sunday. That money has to pay for everything—lunch, dry cleaning, lattes, cabs—and there's no cheating or borrowing from her husband. "If I run out of cash, I'm grounded Saturday night and it's cereal on Sunday." For someone making a comfortable six-figure salary, this obviously takes real determination. Kim also praises online banking as a "godsend. When you can check your balances and make payments in an instant, money becomes less of an abstraction. Now, instead of being shocked by high balances when I get my monthly statement, I go online every few days and transfer money from my checking to my credit cards. This keeps my credit cards always at zero, plus I know exactly how much money I have at all times." And, yet, Kim *still* goes to therapy. "I don't see how anyone can extricate money problems from emotional ones. You can't treat one without addressing the other. They're joined at the core."

The Financial Peter Pan

If you had asked twentysomething Nora where she expected to find herself when she turned 32, she probably would have told you she'd be traveling around the globe in a dance company or finishing her thesis novel for her M.F.A. degree. What she probably would not have said is, "Over $15,000 in credit card debt and asking my parents for money." But today that's exactly the situation Nora is in. Just talking about it causes her to become visibly upset. For Nora, though, even facing the problem represents a huge step forward.

"I just never thought about money," she says. "Never, ever. I think in the back of my mind, I just always assumed somehow things would work out." Yet Nora says she was never in denial about her growing financial problems. "Denial requires an acknowledgement, at least semiconsciously, that there's a problem. I didn't even have that. It was completely off my radar." I ask Nora how that can possibly be. How could she not notice the creeping credit card balances, the chronic shortage of cash, the struggle to pay the bills at the end of the month? Nora swears it never concerned her, and traces the reasons back to her upbringing. "I was in no way spoiled, but I grew up very privileged. We lived in an extremely affluent area, I went to a private school filled with rich kids, and I had a mother who encouraged me to explore my artsy side. Since money is never an issue in that narrow little world, I was never exposed to the downside of not having any. I never feared not having enough. It was just a given that I would."

While Nora's situation may seem a little rarified, her problems transcend her privileged background. Nora doesn't suffer from a sense of entitlement and never relied on a parental safety cushion to fall back on. "I've always worked and I never expected to marry a rich guy. It's much more complicated than that," she insists. Nora feels that both her mother and the world she grew up in shielded her from the value of handling money smartly. "We were encouraged to live *'la vie bohème'*" she says. "So I went to Paris for a few years after college, worked at a fashion magazine, and drank a lot of red wine. The joke being, of course, that to live a nonmaterialistic lifestyle takes a lot of money."

For Nora, the real world came crashing down on her when she was thrown out of work for several months last year. "As long as I could make ends meet, I was still able to slide through life happily oblivious. I paid the minimums. I took my expense checks and used them to pay my personal debts. As long as I could keep the machine running, I assumed everything was fine." When Nora's company abruptly closed, the machine ground instantly to a halt. "I had no money for rent, no money for my credit card debt . . . I was scared." Nora was forced to turn to her mother for a loan, which finally forced her to wake up to her situation. "To go from being fully independent to being a 31-year-old woman who needs to ask Mommy for a handout is humbling, to say the least. It made me reevaluate my own sense of who I really was, that maybe I wasn't quite as mature or as self-reliant as I thought."

Hard as it was for Nora to admit she couldn't get herself out of this mess alone, the realization also marked a real turning point in her relationship with money. The anxiety of going to her mother forced her to acknowledge that the old ways weren't working anymore, if they ever had. She took action. She asked her brother, a Wall Street analyst ("Ironic, I know," she says), to help her with a budget. They spent a Saturday afternoon together learning how to use Quicken to track her finances. Now that she's working again, she keeps her business and personal expenses strictly separate. Most importantly, to help her through her new reality, Nora's in therapy for the first time ever. "I carry a lot of anxiety around now. Anyone carrying $15,000 in credit card debt *should* be anxious. But at least I know now that there is a problem, so I consider this a healthy anxiety. If I had been this clued-in when I was 22, I probably wouldn't find myself in this situation at 32. But a late wake-up call is better than no wake-up call at all."

It's easy to dismiss Nora's problems as those of a dilettante, but there's something deeper going on here. Nora failed to understand that growing up means you can't always live for the moment. As a result, she suffered some very adult consequences. Admittedly, Nora may be an extreme example of the type. After all, few of us spend our mid-twenties in Paris walking the cobblestone streets of the Fifth Arrondissement. However, it's all too common for young people to confuse taking responsibility with relinquishing our dreams. One only has to look at Nora to realize that balance is the best way to hold on to the life you want to live. Nora's now at a job where she works about 60 hours a week and she's slowly paying off her debts. For the time being, the novel she knows she has in her will just have to wait.

The Alpha Spender

Take the well-scrubbed killer from *American Psycho*, strip him of his homicidal impulses, and you've got Eric. A 35-year-old executive at a major consumer goods company, Eric literally wears his success on his sleeve. Shirts from Pink, suits by Jil Sander, Tourneau watch—if you've seen it advertised in the front section of *Vanity Fair*, chances are you've seen it on Eric. He is also, in the words of a friend who's known him since boarding school, "tragically miserable. Eric is the most competitive person I have ever met in my life," he says. "But not competitive in a healthy way, the kind that drives people to better themselves and achieve new personal heights. Eric's all about presentation. He only cares that he has more than everyone else. Actually, that's not true. He only cares that people *think* that he has more than everyone else."

Unlike other people who use materialism to fill an emotional void, Eric's obsession with labels and status is driven by others. Although he hails from a working-class background, his parents managed to send him to a very fancy private school. There, his jealousy and insecurity drove him absolutely crazy and prevented him from developing a strong sense of self.

"Eric is completely shaped by his environment. Despite his intelligence and talent, he feels he can't hold his own."

Eric approached me not too long ago, looking for help. He was charging thousands of dollars on his credit card, and though he was able to pay them off each month, he was left with no savings. He was desperate to get the situation under control. I told him to order a copy of his credit card statements for the past year. We looked over them together, trying to pinpoint exactly where Eric's six-figure (first number not a "1," either) salary was going. I can't say I was surprised at what we found. Eric's shocked response, however, suggested he had been sleepwalking for the past five years. We discovered that a full three-quarters of the charges on Eric's cards went to frivolous luxuries. In dollar terms, it amounted to about $30,000 a year, all on clothes, vacations, and pricey gewgaws!

Once Eric recovered, he saw how keeping up appearances was jeopardizing his future well-being. For Eric, being confronted with hard numbers was all the motivation he needed to change. He got sick when he thought about all that money squandered on overpriced status symbols that could have gone to something more permanent, such as a house or a retirement plan. He now understood why he was finding it harder and harder to keep up with the crowd he wanted to run with. They were all buying houses, opening their own businesses and starting families, while Eric still lived in a rented one-bedroom and leased a car he rarely used.

Eric is slowly mending his ways, but he still has a long way to go before he makes up for time—and money—lost. He would like to start a family, but, incredibly, he fears that he doesn't have the earnings power to support a wife and children. Ironically, Eric's obsession with success and his turbo-charged definition of it are exactly what's kept him from fully achieving it. He needs to learn that life may be a race, but we only win when we compete against ourselves.

The Financial Bulemic

According to her sister Nancy, Eve's success is a mixed blessing. On one hand, the 37-year-old is a very successful proprietor of a small business. On the other, her success enables her to be financially self-destructive without forcing her to get help. Here is a woman who seemingly should have it all—a thriving business, financial independence, breathtaking intelligence—yet she moves through life stalked by an incredible emptiness. Eve goes on wild tears of dramatic overspending, followed by brief periods of chastened frugality. Her sister Nancy wishes Eve would apply her business insights to her own unresolved issues, but she isn't optimistic. "Eve is like a functional alcoholic," Nancy says. "Just because the symptoms aren't visible, it doesn't mean she's not troubled."

Even though their parents are still married, Eve suffers from a blood version of a "stepchild complex." As children, their mother favored her other siblings over Eve. "Eve just pushed all the wrong buttons in our mother," she says. Eve and Nancy come from a very traditional Southern family, where boys were held in higher esteem than girls. Nancy avoided her mother's disapproval by opting for a more traditional life than her older sister. She stayed in the South, married, and today runs a large household. This is a choice their mother respects. Eve moved far away from home and courageously started a business in an industry dominated by men.

As adults approaching middle age, their mother still reinforces her disapproval over Eve's life. Each Christmas their mother sends all of the kids checks. Without fail, Eve's is always lower than everyone else's. Suddenly, Eve is once again the shoved-aside 12-year-old girl. Their mother claims she does this because Eve doesn't need the money. You don't have to be a family therapist to know the truth runs deeper than that. It's her mother's way of registering approval for the other children, while showing disapproval for Eve. For a traditional woman of a certain age, the accomplishments of a single businesswoman mean nothing when there's no ring on her finger.

Eve's internalization of her mother's feelings wreak emotional havoc within her. "She's trying to fill an emotional void with material goods," ventures Nancy, "but on some level she fears this behavior could jeopardize her business. She'll then try to make good by economizing in the most meaningless ways." Like most overspenders, Eve binges on things she has no practical use for. Her palatial home is crammed tight with furniture, art, and collectibles. She owns two cars. Nancy remembers looking in Eve's closets, and flipping through thousands of dollars of clothes from the best department stores, many of them unworn. This is the same woman who delicately opens her business packages so she can reuse the padded envelopes.

Eve can be incredibly generous with others, but then she immediately suffers remorse and tries to right things on her psychological balance sheet. "She worries that she'll be taken advantage of, so if she does something for a friend, she'll then turn the spigot off to make sure that friend sticks around for the right reasons. When she's satisfied they are, she'll turn it back on." Interestingly, Eve's situation improved when she was in a relationship. But the relationship ended, and Eve didn't know how to contend with her grief. The old habits returned in full force. "She has no practice taking emotional risks," says Nancy. "So when Paul broke up with her, it confirmed for her that to open herself up to a relationship meant pain. She went right back to stockpiling. On some level she knows buying things won't satisfy her, but it's like they say—at least they'll never leave her."

The Hoarder

When Marie was a child, she found her mother in the aftermath of a suicide attempt. Thankfully, her mother survived.

Soon after, Marie's family sat her down and tried to explain to the six-year-old that her mother suffered from paranoid schizophrenia, an illness even adults find difficult to comprehend. For Marie, the stress of her home life was too difficult to shoulder. In her own words, she became a "screw-up." The glamorous world of soap operas offered Marie an escape from her harsh reality. Every afternoon, she would camp out in front of the television for hours on end, usually with a joint in hand. Wednesdays were her favorite day, because that meant *Dynasty*. "I had huge delusions of grandeur. I so wanted to be Alexis. She was the epitome of glamor, and nobody owned her. I had a shrine to Joan Collins in my bedroom," she says. "Posters, magazine covers . . . I was obsessed."

Yet Marie didn't have to turn on the television set to get a taste of that world. "I lived in a town that was the East Coast equivalent of Beverly Hills," she explains. Yet despite her family's relative affluence, she grew up believing they were poor. Her father constantly hammered into her the evils of debt and, though emotionally supportive, kept a tight watch over the money. Not surprisingly, she resented his lessons extolling the value of thrift. Marie's high school reflected the status-obsessed values of the community. The kind of BMW you drove mattered, the clothes you wore had to have the right label, kids in school talked about the size of other people's houses. It was that kind of town, and it honed her desire for success. She craved what everyone else had. "My father didn't buy me a car in high school, which I know is not a tragedy, but when everyone else has one, you feel deprived." (Much later she would understand that her father didn't give her a car because he didn't trust his pot-smoking daughter behind the wheel, not because they were poor.) She never wanted to feel inadequate again.

Marie resolved that when she grew up, she would be rich. Until then, she would look and dress the part, but in ways that would never slow her from her goal. "Clothes hang well on me, so I could stick to the classics and still look good. I buy nice things, but I wear them for years and years. I'm just not the kind of woman who would drop $700 on a pair of silly Gucci pants and wear them twice." While she knows that the key to happiness is considerably more complex, she admits to being very in touch with her superficial side. "When I walk down the street, I love knowing that people think I'm rich," she says. While this is not an uncommon to people from modest (or perceived modest) backgrounds, what makes Marie unusual is her militaristic discipline in attaining the future she wants. "My fantasy growing up was always more about driving up in a nice car to a beautiful house with a pool in the back—solid things that will always be there, not another stupid purse. I'm not a *Sex and the City* girl."

Now in her mid-thirties, Marie is spared the credit problems, the retirement anxieties, and the uncertain financial future that many of her friends now face. She instinctively understood early on how debt could trip her up on her way to the Carrington mansion. When she was 22 and making $16,000 at her first job in pricey New York City, her grandmother began giving all of the grandchildren $5,000 gifts each holiday. Marie always banked the check immediately, pretty damn impressive for someone struggling on $300 a week.

While many of her indebted friends would happily trade places with her, Marie's obsession with money brings its own set of miseries. These problems may be a welcome luxury to her more profligate peers, but they have caused Marie to make some decisions detrimental to her long-term happiness. Considering Marie's almost religious attitudes toward saving, for example, it's something of a surprise that she still rents an apartment. But Marie doesn't want to live in the $300,000 house—she wants to fast-forward to the $2,000,000 palace. Consequently, she lost out on the boom of a white-hot real estate market. Since she can't stand the idea of losing money, her investments are absurdly conservative at the time in her life when she should be aggressive.

One also has to wonder what kind of emotional toll obsessing over her finances takes, especially when she confesses, "I didn't choose my career out of any passion for what I do. I just knew I'd be good at it and make money quickly." And she has, though at 36, the strains of working at an unfulfilling job are beginning to show. She still puts in killer hours, but her frustrations have grown with time, and she complains more and more frequently to her husband. A few months ago, she had an anxiety attack so severe she thought she was having a heart attack and was rushed to the emergency room. Yet she won't even consider switching to a more fulfilling career if it means even the smallest pay cut. In some ways, Marie is as trapped in her job as someone in debt. She can easily afford to do something else, but she believes now is not the right time. "I'm hoping that as I become more successful, I'll be less compulsive about money." We'll see.

Debtor's Prison

When asked to describe the house Curtis grew up in, he hesitates for a moment. "Joyless," he responds. Money was in short supply, and his mother, who suffered from severe depression, could not be relied upon as a breadwinner. To keep the family afloat, his father worked seven days a week, although Curtis now believes that his father had more than overtime on his mind. "He wanted to escape from the house, and this was the responsible way for him to do it." Curtis, too, found a way to escape, and while his plan exposed him to many positive influences he would have been denied otherwise, it also planted the seeds of the a financial meltdown he would face in his twenties.

Curtis understood that education was his ticket to the life he wanted, but his local schools were merely average and his family could never afford private school. The resourceful teenager applied to one of his area's elite magnet public schools, which enrolled the best and the brightest from all over the region. Suddenly, Curtis found himself in a classroom filled with the offspring of cardiologists and famous artists. These kids had second homes larger than Curtis' house, yet Curtis says he never felt jealous of the privileged lives of his classmates. "Jealousy implies a competitiveness. But I wasn't competitive with them. It was more like a mystique, or an allure, to me. I loved the aloofness to money they all had. Over time, I adopted that attitude and made it my own."

Surprisingly, Curtis' co-opted attitude toward money played well at home. His parents may have struggled, but the house lacked the domestic tension that often accompanies deprivation. His parents simply accepted living with a certain amount of debt. They weren't reckless or self-indulgent, merely pragmatic. When you can't pay for necessities, you borrow. They always managed to keep household debt at tolerable levels, so it became like background noise. Growing up, Curtis thought owing money was no big deal. Debt was simply part of the fabric of life.

Curtis' parents, perhaps too preoccupied with work and his mother's illness, didn't offer Curtis much financial guidance. They had little money to give him, so after providing the basics, he was on his own. He worked after school and over the summers, and like his parents, didn't save a dime. He spent it on typical teenage junk—music, concerts, clothes. "I made a strong mental connection between earning money and pleasure spending," he says. It was a connection that stayed with him through college where, although he went to school in a small town that offered few outlets to spend money, Curtis always found a way. "Movies, restaurants when I couldn't deal with the meal plan, it didn't matter. I was programmed to get to zero."

This attitude sank Curtis almost as soon as he left college for the real world. Armed with a new credit card and $13,000 in deferred student loans, he quickly dug himself into a steep hole. "It was the first time it all fell on me. I'm not good at prioritizing and organizing. Growing up, debt was such a fact of life, it was easy for me to just ignore it." That's what Curtis did—he literally ignored it. Bills went unopened. Student loans went unpaid. He went on vacation instead of paying the rent. "I'd get irritated just writing a check," he says. Owning an answering machine made it easy to screen out calls from the collection agencies. "I had this feeling that if I just walked away, it would pass."

It's interesting to compare Curtis' experience with Marie's. Despite the strong parallels between their upbringings—troubled mothers, affluent surroundings—Curtis' response to his early years could not diverge more from Marie's. Whereas Marie became almost preternaturally responsible, Curtis rebelled. "I like to flirt with disaster, and not just financially," he says. "Looking over the cliff, one foot dangling over . . . that's me. I love to stretch the boundaries to see how far I can pull them. When you see your father work seven days a week and barely be able to provide, it sends a message—doing the right thing gets you nowhere. I rebelled against that. If you're going to be broke anyway, I figured at least I would have some fun."

Now 33, Curtis is finally beginning to get his act together. Unlike the driven Marie, however, Curtis' desire for financial control derives wholly from an external force. This force even has a name—Louis, Curtis' long-distance boyfriend of over a year. The two have talked seriously about Louis relocating, but Louis has wisely demanded that Curtis reform his ways before he commits to packing up and moving across the country. Louis is Curtis' financial opposite in every way. Debt is anathema, and he knows from experience that both parties need to have similar financial habits to survive as a couple—and it's not going to be Louis who changes. "It took love to get me take my financial situation seriously," says Curtis. "Kind of romantic, if you think about it."

Whatever works, I always say. Curtis and Louis are wise to reach a common understanding *before* they tie the (alternative-lifestyle) knot. Too many couples assume love will conquer all. It's easy to treat money as an afterthought.

Big mistake. The next chapter looks at the many ways couples let money control their marriage instead of the other way around, and shows what you can do to make money a vital and healthy part of your own relationship.

2

Couples Therapy

Five years ago, I made the critical decision to share my life with someone else. As a long-time commitment-phobe, the decision didn't come easily. I weighed the pros against the cons, and asked myself a lot of questions. Was I really ready to surrender my hard-won independence? Was I financially responsible enough to care for someone else? This seemed to be an immutable life change, and frankly, it terrified me. Since divorce was not an option for us, it was strictly a "Till Death Do Us Part" deal. After months of vacillating, I held my breath and finally took the plunge.

I got a dog.

Today, Humbert and I are wildly happy, in no small part because neither of us entered into this domestic partnership lightly. I waited until I was confident that I was emotionally and financially mature enough to sustain a relationship. As for Humbert, I knew he was serious about making it work from the way he gazed at me over the breeder's fence.

If only bipeds put as much thought and care into our relationships with one another as we do with our pets.

You'll often hear people say that buying a house is the biggest financial decision you'll ever make. These people are wrong. Who you're going to live with in that house ultimately impacts your financial future much more than picking the right piece of real estate. Your values, your decision-making, your income, your planning—all of these are heavily influenced by both individuals in the partnership.

Take a look at the graph below. Graph 1 confirms what you've always suspected from reading the Sunday wedding announcements in the *New York Times*: we're waiting longer and longer to walk down the aisle. To my mind, that's a positive trend. Marriage is like fame—few young people really know how to handle it. Settling down later in life allows us to first grow into the person we were meant to be. As we learn to rely on ourselves and answer to no one, we become more healthy, self-aware people. By the time we finally choose Mr. or Ms. Right, most of us have notched more years of independent living under our belts than our parents and grandparents combined. This independence can bring a healthy maturity to a relationship, but it also creates additional challenges for a young couple.

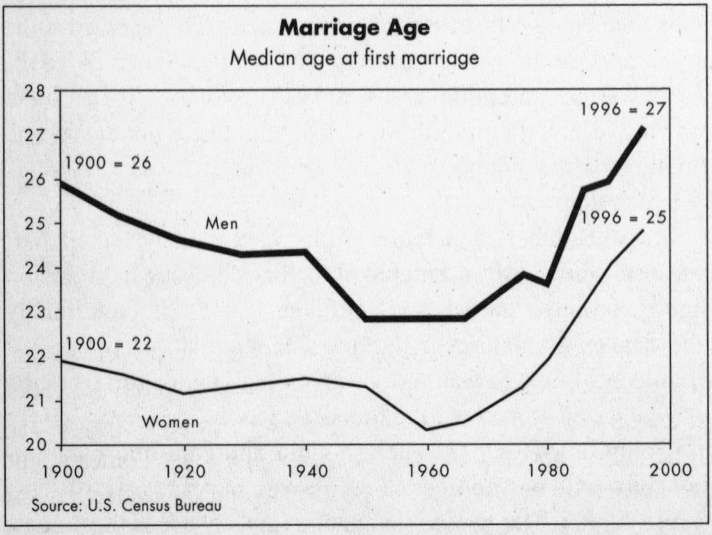

Of course, late weddings aren't the only way Marriage 2.0 differs from earlier models. Growing up, there's a pretty good chance your mother didn't work. And if she did, you probably had a lot of friends with stay-at-home moms. Now think about your married friends today. How many of them have a non-working spouse? I made a list of mine and came up with exactly one.

Unfortunately, two incomes don't usually translate to twice the standard of living. Factor in increased child care costs, a possible "marriage penalty" tax, spiraling housing costs, maybe an extra car, etc. and most couples find themselves working twice as hard just to stay even with the way their parents lived. Is it any surprise, then, that so many marriages buckle and collapse under the stress?

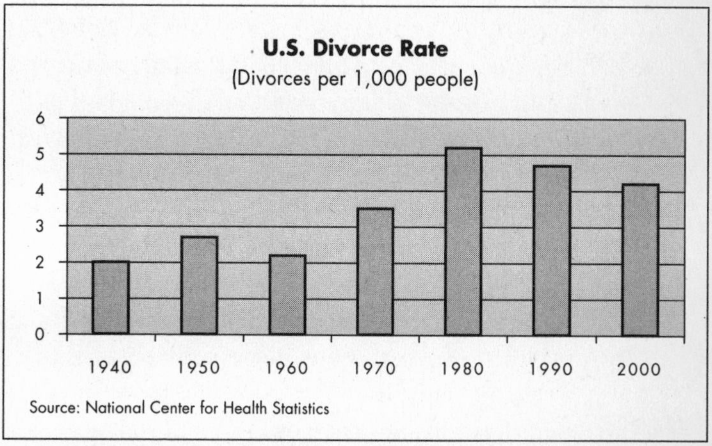

It's never been more difficult to balance marriage, money and family. Although young couples have known this for years, the media just now seems to be catching on. A novel by a first-time author about a woman trying to juggle her domestic and professional responsibilities becomes a runaway bestseller. The simmering tension between working mothers and stay-at-homes gets a national magazine cover story. A presidential adviser leaves her Washington power post, whisks her family back to Texas, and becomes a lightning rod for the dilemma that many powerful career women face. What does it all mean?

Although thirtysomethings are hardly the first generation to struggle with the changing rules of work and home, today young couples are asked to shoulder responsibilities that dwarf those of previous generations. According to one study, between 1989 and 1998 the workload of middle-income couples rose by 246 hours per year. That's more than six full-time work weeks added to an already harried schedule. As one woman said of her marriage when I told her this, "No wonder we can't get ahead. We're too exhausted from making a living to have a life."

You've probably seen the divorce studies that claim money is the number one reason marriages in this country fail. That blows my mind. We live in the richest country in the world, and yet people routinely allow their most treasured relationships to be destroyed by mammon. Clearly, lack of money isn't the real culprit. (Otherwise, a lot more people from Bangladesh to Brazil would be calling 1-800-DIVORCE.)

So if the issue isn't economic survival, why did over a million couples call it quits this year? There is, of course, no pat answer, but from the interviews conducted for this book and from my own informal observations, I see differences emerging between mutually satisfying marriages and troubled ones. Those in content relationships treat money as an integral part of the marriage and use it to foster intimacy, trust, and growth. Those suffering constant strife, however, adopt the opposite stance.

These people fear money. Often this attitude stems directly from the ways in which their own parents used money against each other. Though many recall the unhappiness and anxiety these conflicts created in their childhood homes, they have nonetheless absorbed their parents' attitudes. Like their healthier counterparts, these people also recognize the enormous power of money. Unfortunately, they view it as a power that can only undermine and destroy. Either they try to neutralize money as a force in the relationship, which is impossible, or they use it as a weapon against the person they love.

In this chapter I've taken the experiences of couples from all different walks of life and distilled them into five guiding principles. You will find that most of these principles are nothing more than good old-fashioned common sense. But as anyone who's been in a relationship knows, emotions very often hijack common sense. We end up rejecting sound judgment in exchange for the more expedient, easier, and sometimes just plain stupid decision. The lessons here are both universal and timeless. So timeless, in fact, that if you go back 2,500 years, you'll find they were first uttered by Aesop, the preternaturally wise slave and cherished favorite of third-grade teachers everywhere. I'd say that qualifies as standing the test of time. And while I can't tell you what Aesop would have said about tax shelters or the stock market, I can promise that following these five fundamental principles will help strengthen every couples' approach to money.

* * *

A farmer grew tired of listening to his two sons fight. He begged them to try and resolve their differences, but the two continued to butt heads. Finally, things got so tense, he decided to teach them both a lesson. He summoned them to the wood shack. Thinking their father had a grand pronouncement in mind, the two sons went. He handed them a bundle of firewood and told them to break it in half. The sons laughed at the request, but decided they would entertain the old man. Strong as the boys were, they could not break the sticks in the bundle. The father then untied the bundles and handed each son one stick at a time. The sticks easily snapped in their hands.

"So you see!" said the father, "If you stay together, no one can hurt you. But if you act alone, you will be easy to defeat."

Moral: When two act as one, both become stronger.

If you're married, think back to when you walked down the aisle on that happiest of days. Do you remember what was going through your head? Was it "OK, he paid for the cake, but I paid for the bouquet. His parents got the caterer, but mine took care of the catering hall. But the caterer cost more. Good thing he got the band. Hmmm . . . how much was the band again?" Of course not. Marriage is supposed to be about coming together—not worrying about how to split the check. Yet many of us enter this holiest of unions thinking, "Every man (or woman) for himself!"

It's not hard to understand the roots of this. With one of every two marriages ending in Splitsville, many people enter marriage with a backup plan in place. Today, few hear the words "happily ever after" without at least a healthy dose of skepticism. That's why God made pre-nups, right? But I'm not talking about protecting yourself should things fall apart. That's not acting as an individual—that's just being smart. A pre-nup can keep an already ugly situation from getting uglier. It strips the supercharged emotions out of the cold, hard task of cleaving your assets. We've all heard the horror stories of a wife being left with nothing because everything was in hubby's name. It's tragic to think that two people once joined by love can treat each other this way, but it happens. A reality check doesn't mean you love your partner any less.

When I say acting individually, I'm talking about being half of a couple and still behaving like a single person. Elaine is typical of this phenomenon. After a string of long-term relationships, she married Mitchell at age 34. Though she had lived with her husband for five years before finally tying the knot, she still found it difficult to think as a couple. She insisted on strict financial segregation. Elaine's reluctance stemmed from deep-rooted emotional issues involving trust and control. In her words, finances became an extension of those issues. "There was definitely a feeling of what's mine is mine and what's yours is yours," she says. She also had serious concerns about Mitchell's earnings potential. He was in the process of changing careers, and his future income was uncertain.

Fortunately for Elaine, she had a very patient husband. "Mitch isn't bothered by these issues, so he didn't fully understand them. He hoped that in time I would just become more comfortable with idea of being married." He first suggested that the two of them consolidate their credit card debt by transferring it all to one low-interest card. Both could contribute to paying it off, and soon Elaine forgot exactly who owed what. Next, Mitch did the same with their student loan debt, even though he owed less on his than she did. Mitch made getting out of debt a priority, and by working together with Elaine he showed her what the two could accomplish.

It was a gradual process, but today Elaine is almost converted to the wisdom of sharing. Old habits die hard, however, and once in a while her old self resurfaces. Recently she inherited a considerable amount of money from a grandparent. Not a fortune, but enough, as she says, "to make a life change." This was over a year ago, and still Elaine cannot bring herself to put Mitchell's name on the account. She understands the fundamental unfairness of this—in one year he earns more than the inheritance (and, now, more than she does), yet he shares everything. "It's funny," she says. "After I got this money, my father pleaded with me to keep it separate from the rest of our money. It gave me a pretty in-your-face reminder where my attitude comes from. I don't want a marriage like my parents, so ironically, I think he inadvertently helped Mitchell's cause." Mitchell, for his part, is displaying his usual patience. In time,

Elaine knows she'll come around. "He's accepted that this is my particular 'thing.' He just lets me come around to his way of thinking on my own terms. I'm sure at times he gets frustrated with my hesitation, but he understands I grew up in a house with some seriously unhealthy attitudes toward money. He didn't. With our backgrounds, we won't automatically meet in the middle."

Elaine and Mitch are living proof that starkly different approaches to money can be reconciled. Though she's made great strides, she still has some work ahead of her. Elaine and Mitchell don't have a will or a pre-nup. Neither had significant assets when they married, so perhaps in their case skipping the pre-nup is excusable. But now that they've got six figures sitting in the bank and a two-year-old son, a will is long overdue. Elaine credits procrastination and their respective clean bills of health, but recognizes the risk in not dealing with it.

Taking care of your partner in the event of the unthinkable may be an unpleasant thing to contemplate, but it simply cannot be neglected. When you don't have a will, you are not acting as a couple. Your responsibility to each other extends beyond your natural life. No one likes to think about death, but it's going to happen whether we think about it or not. Roughly two-thirds of the people in this country die without leaving a will. This creates additional trauma for their survivors. Ask any widow who's had to endure hours of court appearances and paperwork to protect her estate after her husband died. Dying intestate (as it's called) is perhaps the most extreme example of letting money divide you as a couple, rather than unite you.

If you've been putting off making a will for any reason, you *must* change your way of thinking. Don't think about the morbid aspects of preparing for the inevitable. Instead, view it as an integral stone in the foundation of your commitment to one another. Sit your partner down, explain why you can't put this off any longer, and make an appointment with a lawyer. I guarantee that after leaving his office, you and your partner won't be depressed. Instead, you'll feel relieved for taking ultimate responsibility for the person you love.

* * *

Fable: While tending his garden, a man's dog had fallen down a well. This man loved his dog, so he rushed down the well to save it. But the frightened dog, seeing his master rush at him, assumed his owner was going to push him down even further. When the man reached for the dog, the dog bit his owner's hand. The man pulled his bleeding hand back and climbed out, complaining:

"Fine, then. Why should I help him when he clearly wants to starve to death?"

Moral: The best intentions can be misunderstood without open communication.

We're taught from a very young age that civilized people don't talk about money. Most of us learned early on that around the dinner table, conversations about money were strictly off-limits. Money is private, we're told. Only the vulgar and Donald Trump consider it an acceptable topic of conversation. In my own house, money came up only when we asked for something. Then we were told to go out and work for it.

There's a big difference between boasting about what you have and discussing how money can enrich both your lives. I'm a strong advocate for making money a more active part of every couple's life. Let's think for a minute about some of the words that come to mind when describing a satisfying marriage. Words like solid, secure, and steady. Note how these words could just as easily be used to describe healthy finances. Let's be real—great sex isn't enough to sustain endless love. If it were, Pam and Tommy Lee would still be together. Real commitment and intimacy come from open communication between you and your partner. When you know exactly what the other is thinking. Wrong assumptions won't be made, silences won't be misread, and resentments won't grow unchecked.

Now, I'm not naïve. I'm not claiming that communication will lead to unmitigated marital bliss. Fights and disagreements come with the domestic—and financial—territory. But conflict gets a worse rap than it deserves. Approached correctly, conflict can actually foster intimacy rather than destroy it. A Manhattan-based therapist I know sees a large number of otherwise strong-willed, type-A folks, who nevertheless run scared when faced with conflict of any sort. He teaches his clients that friction isn't dangerous to a relationship—avoiding it is. This therapist explains that healthy relationships rarely travel in a straight line. Conflict temporarily pulls two people apart and forces them to realign. When they resolve the issue at hand, they emerge stronger. Every resolved conflict, no matter how small, strengthens them as a unit and enables them to withstand even greater strife next time.

But how, you ask, does this relate to money? In the last chapter you saw the inseparable connection between emotion and money. Emotions are the DNA of a relationship, so it follows that money plays a crucial role in determining the emotional state of the union. Yet many couples don't see the connection. Like Nora, the Paris artiste in the last chapter, these couples deny money's role in creating a lasting bond. I say, if you don't make money a regular part of the marital dialogue, the silence will be deafening.

Morgan and Peter have been married for five years. With Peter unemployed and a baby on the way, money is a major issue in their relationship right now. Yet the two of them have erected a Great Wall of Silence regarding all things financial. "We just can't talk about it. I get too upset," says Morgan. Peter lost his six-figure job at a dot.com six months ago and with the job market so bleak, he's turned instead to graduate school. As Peter was the former breadwinner the couple will have to endure serious belt-tightening for the foreseeable future. Yet Morgan

Paying Retail, Lying Wholesale

When asked to cite an example of a financial trick they're guilty of, many women confess to fibbing about the true cost of a new purchase to avoid conflict. (I say "women" because no man I spoke to would admit to this. Either they're simply more honest with their spouses or just better at lying to interviewers.) Whether lopping off a zero or dividing the actual price by two, many women prefer to knock a few dollars off when they get home instead of at the cash register.

In the canon of whoppers, lying about the number on the price tag is hardly the biggest transgression. Still, it's a habit that can spill over to more critical areas of a marriage. Better to ask yourself why you feel the need to lie. Is the item truly overpriced? Or maybe your husband just doesn't understand that $450 is a perfectly acceptable price for a pair of shoes. Whatever. Ultimately, marriage is give-and-take. He won't agree with all of your priorities, just as you won't agree with all of his. As long as neither of you is endangering your household's finances, you're both better off learning to tolerate each other's spending quirks than resorting to white lies.

Besides, if he's smart, he'll keep his mouth shut. This way, when he walks through the door carrying a $5,000 Bang & Olufsen stereo, you'll have no choice but to do the same.

and Peter avoid talking about money now more than ever, when the time has never been more crucial to coordinate and focus their efforts. It's a form of financial hibernation, and it's beginning to tear at the seams of the marriage. What should be an exciting and joyful of time for the parents-to-be is instead fraught with anxiety. Says Morgan: "We live entirely separate financial lives. I have no idea how much money he owes and he has no idea how much credit card debt I carry. This might be hard for someone else to understand, but for us, revealing debt would be way more intimate than any sex act."

Morgan, who doesn't mince words, confesses to also being guilty of "castration shopping." Because she can't accept her financial situation, she's turned to her mother to pump up her standard of living, though she is deeply conflicted about it. "My whole family has always been very generous. It's how we show love and give comfort. So now, my mother is buying stuff for the house and the baby because we can't afford it. It's demeaning and emasculating for Peter. I mean, he's thirty-seven years old. But she loves it. We've become my mother's hobby."

Even the most ordinary decisions couples make together become charged with Morgan and Peter. For example, with the baby coming the couple decided they needed a larger apartment. Perfectly reasonable. They even acted responsibly by agreeing to set a limit they could afford. So far, so good. Then Morgan got call from their broker at work. A beautiful rental had just come on the market. It would be gone before the end of the day. If Morgan wanted to look at it, she would have to drop everything and meet her at the apartment right now. Morgan dashed out of the building, fell in love with the apartment and pounced on it—even though it was more than the rent the couple had mutually agreed upon. Morgan could have called her husband and discussed it with him, but she didn't. She was simply afraid that her more cautious, practical husband would veto the higher rent, so she didn't give him the option. She avoided conflict. This decision might have landed the couple a nicer apartment (albeit one they can barely afford), but it also left one half of the couple feeling, once again, like an unequal partner.

* * *

Fable: One summer day a grasshopper was frolicking in a meadow, chirping and singing. An ant strolled by, grunting and groaning as it pushed an ear of corn to the anthill.

"That looks like hard work," observed the grasshopper. "Come play with me instead."

"Winter will be here before you know it," replied the ant. "I am storing enough food now, so we can survive the cold months. I suggest you do the same."

"Who can think about winter now?" asked the grasshopper. "We've got plenty of food right now." But the ant continued pushing the corn to the faraway anthill. Winter finally came and the grasshopper had no food. As it slowly starved to death, it saw the plump ants feasting on the corn they had stored over the summer.

Moral: The time to prepare for the future is the present.

This rather morbid tale highlights the importance of planning. In many ways it is an extension of the fable before it, because without open communication, planning becomes impossible. But while talking freely with your partner about money will foster trust and intimacy, it's making a plan where you want to be in ten, twenty, even thirty years that allows those feelings to grow unimpeded.

You can't plan for the future if you don't have well-defined goals. While it sounds so obvious I feel silly even saying it, there are many, many thirtysomething couples out there living for the moment and not much else. Clearly they haven't learned this critical rule of financial planning. Either that, or else some goals feel so unattainable or distant that couples give up before even trying. Whatever the reason, the consequences—both emotional and financial—are too great to ignore.

No matter how remote your dreams may seem, identifying them is a critical component of any healthy relationship. Human beings need purpose and direction. Couples are the same. Nothing breeds anxiety more quickly than the feeling of being adrift and aimless, and your financial journey is no exception. When neither of you knows where you're headed, there's no way to measure your progress. The resulting frustration can seep into a relationship in many different ways. Vague feelings of dissatisfaction may begin to plague you, although superficially you and your partner are on solid financial ground.

Gayle and Danny married four years ago. Unfortunately, each brought their financial phobias with them. Gayle feared taking responsibility for her finances to the point where she admits she didn't open her banking statements for a solid year. For his part, Danny worked in a notoriously low-paying profession. He dreaded the possibility that he would never make enough money to have the lifestyle that his friends all seemed to be easing into. The result: both continued down the paths of their old habits, their hopes for the future never articulated.

Danny began to intuit that things were growing static. "Our situation was never dire," he says. "We were even saving some money, although it was in a savings account, which in hindsight was foolish." But Danny felt a feeling of unease beginning to creep into the marriage. Since everything else was going so well, he was able to isolate the problem. He figured out that they needed to start working toward something real. "It was a marriage firing on seven pistons instead of eight. Everything else was going perfectly, but I realized we had to address our unwillingness to push forward, or it would create bigger problems."

To put Gayle in a comfortable mood, Danny cooked her an elaborate home-cooked meal on a Saturday night, and then gently explained his concerns to her. "I wanted her to be completely relaxed, so I made her favorite meal. After dinner, we cracked open a bottle of wine and sat in the living room together. I took out a pad and drew four columns that listed our income, our expenses, what we had saved so far, and what we could be saving. I first showed her that we could be much smarter with our money, and then explained why I thought we hadn't been. There was no blame on my part or hers. Keeping it positive was really important. I didn't want Gayle to get depressed or anxious."

It worked. With his partner now engaged and not defensive, Danny talked about where they saw themselves in the coming years. They took turns writing down what they would like to accomplish. Neither wants to rent forever, so they first put a house on the list. Gayle wants to work for herself one day, so they next added "Gayle's business." They are undecided about children, so "kids" got a question mark. "It grew to be a pretty big wish list, but we're both optimistic and resourceful people. As long as we had something concrete to work toward, we feel in time we'll get it."

Danny marks that conversation as their financial turning point. "We closed our savings account and moved all of the money into a mutual fund." The couple realized that at their current rate of savings, by the time they had enough to pursue their goals, they would be too old to fully enjoy them. Saving money became a top priority, and today they save at a rate that would put a Japanese household to shame. (They're big savers over in Tokyo.) Both work on salary plus commission, so they try to use their base to cover living expenses and bank the entire commission. "We pretend the commission part of the paycheck doesn't exist," explains Gayle. "It goes immediately into the Fidelity funds."

Gayle says having something tangible to look forward to reinvigorated her outlook. "We were beginning to slide into a rut . . . getting up every day . . . going to work . . . with no real direction. Now, we'll drive by a house we love and think that one day we can live in a house like that. We can daydream without feeling we're setting ourselves up for disappointment. If we just stay on course we'll eventually get what we want."

* * *

Fable: One day an injured frog in a marsh announced to all the animals:

"I am a doctor and I can cure anything!"
Hearing this, a fox called back:
"Why should we trust you when you can't even cure your own limp?"

Moral: Anyone can call himself a professional financial planner. Investigate your planner's background before turning over your money.

If you needed open heart surgery, you wouldn't look in the Yellow Pages and choose your doctor based on the size of his ad. So why do so many couples choose their financial planner based on little more than the prestige of his office address? Choosing the person with whom you will trust your life savings is almost as important as the doctor you choose to save your life. Yet it's shocking how remarkably careless people can be when hiring the person who, after their own spouse, is likely to have the greatest impact on their financial future.

Financial planners aren't for everyone. I know plenty of determined Do-It-Yourselfers who wouldn't dream of letting another human being near their money. And for a certain type of person, that's perfectly fine. But if you and your spouse aren't likely to spend your Saturdays poring over finance magazines and investment books, hiring a financial planner is something to consider. As we get older, our financial picture tends to grow more complicated, and you may be overlooking ways to maximize your money. It becomes increasingly time-consuming to stay on top of all the investing and tax opportunities to hold onto as much of your cash as possible. The days of the 1040EZ are a faded, distant memory.

The best way to find a good financial planner is to ask someone who uses one. Talk to various friends or co-workers about their experiences with their planner. This can save you valuable time with the vetting process. However, it is important to remember not to take these endorsements at face-value. People often exaggerate results in order to make themselves look smart for hiring the right person. It's human nature. Who wants to admit that they hired someone who's losing money for them? If you've ever had to endure someone at a dinner party bragging about his brilliant stock pick, you know exactly what I'm talking about. He may have picked *one* winner. Dig a little deeper, though, and you'll find out about the five duds he bought before that.

Before you set up a consultation, do a background check. Ten years ago this required considerable legwork. Now, with the Internet, it takes seconds. Three sites can help. The first, nasdr.com, is run by the National Association of Securities Dealers. The site provides the adviser's job history for the past ten years (be suspicious of frequent job changes) as well as the states in which he or she is licensed. Click on "Disclosure Events" to learn if the adviser has been convicted of a felony or ever filed for bankruptcy. (*Big* no-no.) If he has, steer clear.

Nasaa.org (North American Securities Administrators Association) requires a few more clicks to get what you want, but they provide links to state regulators, which can provide you with more detailed disciplinary records than NASD.

Lastly, to check the licensed credentials of a financial planner, go to cfp-board.org. This is the site of the Certified Financial Planner Board of Standards. They will confirm the status of a Certified Financial Planner.

Now that you've done your homework, the next step is to make an appointment with the adviser you are considering. It's a good idea to go armed with a list of prepared questions you have. Four of the most salient:

- **How Are You Compensated?** Financial planners make their money three ways. Traditionally, they worked on

commission, and many still do. This means that every time she buys or sells an investment for you, she takes a percentage. This system works very well provided you have a portfolio of reasonably stable investments and your planner is honest. Unfortunately, this is not always the case. Unethical advisers will often manipulate your investments for the sole purpose of generating commissions. Though illegal, "churning" (as the practice is called) is difficult to prove, which makes it all the more tempting to the unscrupulous.

This is not to suggest that commission-based advisers are an inherently untrustworthy breed. Most will treat your money as they do they're own. But it's wise to exercise a little oversight with your accounts until you feel you can trust your planner. Be wary of annual commissions that exceed 2 percent of your total assets under his control.

Personally, I prefer either a "fee-based" or a "fee-only" adviser. Fee-based advisers receive a combination of commission and fees. Fee-only advisers charge either an hourly rate or, more commonly, a flat percentage of the assets under management. With this system, you won't get any nasty surprises. You agree to his fee (usually in the area of 1 to 2 percent) and it's deducted from your account. Simple. I like fee-based or fee-only advisers because their interests are totally aligned with yours. If your portfolio goes up, they make more money. If it declines, they make less. Unfortunately, many fee-only advisers won't manage anything less than several hundred thousand dollars. That's a problem for most new couples starting out, so if you're sold on a fee-only adviser, you may have to search a little harder.

- **Will you provide references from other clients?** Even if the person across the desk comes highly recommended from someone you know, check out the other clients' experiences. If he's unwilling to cough up a few contacts, it probably means none of them have anything nice to say. Find someone else. (By the way, don't fall for the "confidentiality" excuse. You're not asking to examine someone else's net worth. Most satisfied clients are happy to endorse their advisers, if only in the hope the adviser will return the favor and give their portfolio a little more attention.)
- **What is your approach to financial planning?** A good financial adviser considers the whole picture, not just the cash you have on hand to invest. Say, for example, you have $15,000 you want to invest in the stock market. Some financial advisers would ask nothing further and invest it for you. A better adviser would consider other factors, such as high-interest debt you might be carrying. You'd almost always be better off paying down those 18 percent credit card balances than taking a flyer on the market and a good planner will look out for this kind of thing.

Be wary of certain biases a prospective planner may have. Depending on the world they come from, they may lean toward a portfolio overweighted in their area of expertise. For example, don't be surprised if you choose a planner with a ChFC title after her name and she suggests life insurance or annuities as investment vehicles. While that may in fact be the right strategy for you, she may also simply be pushing those investment options because her background is limited. (See chart below for a list of the various financial planner titles and what they mean.)

Know Your P's & Q's: Common Adviser Titles

Title	What It Stands For	What It Means
C.F.A.	Chartered Financial Analyst	Specializes in securities
C.F.P.	Certified Financial Planner	Comprehensive financial planning
C.P.A.	Certified Public Accountant	Accounting expertise
C.I.M.C.	Certified Investment Management Consultant	Identifies good mutual funds and money managers
ChFC	Chartered Financial Consultant	Financial planners with insurance background
G.S.R.	General Securities Representative	A broker trained only in investment products

- What are your credentials and experience? You should know more about your planner than the initials after his name and what you find out on nasdr.com. Ask him how long he's been a financial planner. What does he consider his areas of expertise? For example, does he specialize in retirement planning, or does he cater to clients looking for high-risk/high-growth investments? His experience should suit your goals.

Remember, there is no question too naïve or simple for an adviser to answer. It's your money we're talking about. You deserve to have every one of your questions answered patiently, thoroughly and honestly. If you leave the consulation feeling anything less than completely comfortable, I strongly recommend that you go with your gut and keep searching. Your relationship with your financial planner is not unlike your relationship with your therapist. It will be far more beneficial for you if the chemistry between you is as strong as the advice.

* * *

Fable: A winemaker lay on his deathbed and called his children to gather round him. He wanted to discuss his will, he told them. Gasping for breath, he said, "I am not long for this world, but, I have taken care of all of you. You will find a prosperous future hidden deep in the vineyard."

Shortly after, the winemaker died. The children, remembering their father's dying words, assumed their father had buried his wealth somewhere in the vineyard. They tilled the vineyard from one end to the other looking for the riches their father promised them. They found nothing. But the vineyard, so well tended, gave its best harvest ever.

Moral: Teach your children the rewards of work and it will be the best gift you can give them.

Growing up, my father did his best to teach us what we needed to know to get through life. He told us that he didn't care what we did for a living as long as it made us happy, and emphasized how important self-confidence would be to achieve anything meaningful in life. Most importantly, he told us not to even think about using his car while he was away because he had written down the mileage and he would be checking it when he got back. I don't take any of these lessons for granted. The first helped me decide what I wanted to do with my life, the second helped me get it. The last lesson kept him from killing me at age 19. I will always be grateful for that.

What he did not teach us about was money. I don't blame him for this. He is hardly the first parent to subscribe to the theory that that money is not an appropriate topic of discussion in front of the kids. Many parents believe that the rules of money will be lost on minds preoccupied with Little League, afterschool television, and British pop music. They assume that kids will be careful with money when it's their own *(wrong!)*. And, failing that, they believe that if they give their kids a decent education, financial success will follow. But as many of us know firsthand, a solid income doesn't guarantee security. It's not how much you make; it's what you do with it.

Teaching your kids the values and skills they need to prosper is one of the most important responsibilities of a parent. Not only do you raise savvier kids, but your relationship with your partner benefits as well. First and most obviously, you won't have to worry about supporting your deadbeat kid when he's forty. That's no fun for anybody, and it happens way more often than you think. I know a fully capable 39-year-old woman who lives in a Mommy-subsidized apartment, works at a job Mommy got for her, and charges high-priced designer clothes on Mom's credit card. Do you really want to spend your retirement paying for your child's winter wardrobe? I doubt it.

How early is too early? For my money, there is no such thing. Hillary, the married mother of Josh, has already started giving her three-year-old son rudimentary money lessons. Growing up, her parents kept her completely in the dark about money. As an adult, she was intimidated by all things financial and squandered some of her prime earnings years because of it. She doesn't want Josh to grow up making the same mistakes. Already she's familiarizing him with the concept of money, which is no easy feat with a hyperactive three-year-old. When they go to stores together, she has Josh hand the money to the cashier and take the change. She is teaching him that when he wants a new toy, there is a real cost attached. "He's obsessed with this one particular train set," Hillary cites as an example. "Well, there are probably 100 different models of train cars in the set. He wants them all, of course, but we're teaching him that these trains don't just magically appear. They come from Mommy and Daddy and there's a real cost to them." Hillary uses the trains to reward good behavior. "We want Josh to understand the concept of 'earning' something. Obviously, he can't work in the traditional sense, but this way he grasps the concept of 'working' toward something. He'll learn he won't just get something because he wants it."

Josh's financial future isn't the only beneficiary here. With both partners participating in something as seemingly basic as a three-year-old's introduction to money, both Hillary and her husband Marc feel not only more invested in his overall future, they also have a safe arena for discussion and sharing ideas. "It's definitely helped us in other areas of our relationship," says Hillary. "There are so many different approaches to raising a child. Josh's financial education is something we both feel strongly about, and we're always bouncing ideas off of each other for new ways to teach him. It showed us how much nicer it is for us when Marc and I are on the same page."

3

Your $249,180* Bundle of Joy

We all know that old high school health class exercise aimed at reducing teenage pregnancy. Girls are given an egg and told to carry it around for a week. They are responsible for that egg 24 hours a day. For seven days a week they must take it with them everywhere: to school, to the mall, to cheerleading practice—there are no vacations from egg-care. You can imagine by week's end, there are a lot of cracked eggs.

Instead of fancy china, sometimes I think newlyweds should be handed a carton of eggs.

Nothing impacts your life as dramatically as bringing another life into this world. Unless you are very, very wealthy or have parents who live next door and are simply *dying* for grandchildren, every aspect of your life will change—your finances, your career choices, and how you spend your so-called "down time."

Even prospective couples who prepare themselves well for parenthood can't quite grasp the sea-change that bringing home

* Estimated cost of raising a child to the age of 17, according to U.S. Department of Agriculture. Figure does not include college expenses.

Baby inevitably entails. As a friend of mine told me, "Now I know why new mothers form this instant bond, even if they have nothing else in common. This is one experience that can only be understood by someone else who's going through it."

With the cost of raising a child increasing at a rate that leaves inflation in the dust, it is more crucial than ever for parents-to-be to prepare themselves for the reality of the next 18 years of their lives. This chapter explores your options for child care, career, and education—three areas that necessitate making seemingly daunting choices. Admittedly, for many families there is no such thing as an ideal solution. If you haven't yet let go of the myth of "having it all," chances are you will after reading the next 20 pages. Indeed, some of the facts and figures I've found may make you wonder how anybody brings another life into this world without sliding into Chapter Eleven.

Where there's a will there's a way. Today's parents have more choices and flexibility than ever before to mold a plan to suit their family's individual needs. New parenthood can be an overwhelming, and yes, even frightening experience. For all the elation to be found in picking the perfect name and shopping for tiny socks and t-shirts, many parents fear that their lives will be restricted in ways they can't even imagine. That's understandable, but it's also not productive. Educating yourself about the many options parents have today will help eliminate the anxiety surrounding your brand new 8.2 pound, 3 A.M. wake-up call.

Working Girl: Making a Living Beyond the 9-to-5 Grind

In the (very) old days, most middle-class families didn't have to contend with issues of who would actually do most of the real work associated with raising kids. (By real work, I don't mean contributing a couple of chromosomes and calling it a day. I mean wiping baby puke from the backseat of the car and keeping Mommy's jewelry out of tiny mouths.) The division of labor was set in stone: Dad went to work each morning, and Mom tended the brood. Alternatives were almost unthinkable. My own grandfather worked three jobs supporting his family so my grandmother could stay home and take care of the house and kids. (With three "spirited" boys running around a 2700-square-foot house, it's open to debate who had the harder job.) Only after her last child was in high school did she even consider taking a job. A working mom was simply unheard of in those days. Back then, unless the country was at war, a working mother was someone to be pitied, not admired.

Flash forward 50 years or so. While many mothers (and quite a few fathers) choose to stay home to see Junior through his formative years, most parents today don't have that option. The economics simply don't work for today's middle-class aspirations. So, many parents bite the bullet, fork over a big chunk of their combined salaries to child care, and wind up exhausted, financially static, and guilty.

Many employers have realized that the old model isn't exactly conducive to retaining inspired, productive, and fully-awake employees. In the past ten years, many companies have shown tremendous willingness to work with employees to juggle the demands of work and home. Unfortunately, many people assume their employer won't work with them to accommodate their needs, or they fear that their career will derail unless they spend 50-plus hours under the boss' nose. Neither is necessarily true. With no less than your sanity at stake, it's worth considering some alternatives to the Monday through Friday grind.

Flextime

Never a morning person, I remember grumpily setting my alarm clock all through high school for 5:50 A.M., the whole time imagining how much better life would be if I could just start the day two hours later. As an adult, I discovered that most office jobs have the same rigid, unbending approach to scheduling as my local school district. Fortunately, with the introduction of *flextime*, some employers are relaxing their approach. They are realizing that allowing employees to set their own schedules often results in increased productivity. One of the most successful workplace innovations of the nineties, flextime is a concept so brilliant in its simplicity that many working parents can't imagine life without it.

You and your partner can save a bundle on child care when both of you use flextime to stagger your work schedules. If one of you can stay home in the morning with your kid and the other can come home early, you can shave hours off of your nanny's bills. (It's also, of course, a great way to spend more time with your kid. Who can forget that famous story of little Ron Reagan, Jr., growing up believing his nanny was his real mother? Quality time only compensates for so much, I guess.)

Flextime doesn't allow you to cut back the actual hours you spend at the office. That's the bad news. The good news is you can adjust your work week to accommodate your home responsibilities. You can take your kid to nursery school, attend the 9:00 A.M. parent-teacher conference, and still hold down a full-time job with its accompanying benefits.

To accommodate the needs of each employer, flextime policies vary considerably from office to office. Some companies allow you to come and go as you please, as long as you work the required number of hours each week. If you work for one of these companies, don't ever leave! Most employers won't grant you that degree of latitude, but many will still allow considerable flexibility in designing your own schedule. They might let you come in early and leave early, or start late and work into the evening. Most will, however, require that you keep your schedule consistent.

Compressed Work Week

In this type of arrangement, you work full-time hours on a part-time schedule. How, you ask, is that possible? With a *compressed work week*, you agree to work a longer work day in exchange for a shorter work week. Instead of the traditional 9-to-5, Monday through Friday grind, for example, you commit to working 8–6, Monday through Thursday. Note in both schedules the actual number of hours worked is the same (40), but the latter example gives you Fridays off to spend more time with your family. There are some solid advantages to working a compressed work week, but it's not right for everyone.

First, you must decide if you have the stamina to work an extended day. Many people, even if they're swimming in Starbucks, simply stop being productive after the eighth hour. If that describes you, your performance may suffer and your boss will certainly take notice. Instead, you might consider the so-called 5–4/9 schedule, which requires alternating five nine-hour days with a less rigorous week of four nine-hour days.

You should also consider the impact that a long workday may have on your family life. It may not be easy finding a baby-sitter willing to watch your kids from sunrise to sundown. Also, if you come home exhausted and irritable at the end of each day at the office, you are probably not doing your spouse and kids a favor by compressing your work week.

On the plus side, who doesn't love a three-day weekend? Imagine getting off for Lincoln's birthday 52 times a year. Pretty sweet, right? Your family can take more short vacations, and you get 72 glorious hours away from Annoying Stan in the next cubicle.

If you decide the compression route is right for you, again I strongly suggest crafting a proposal that reassures the boss he won't have a less productive employee on his hands. Also, most people probably shouldn't take Monday as their day off. First, many paid U.S. holidays already fall on a Monday. Secondly, in my experience the goals and tone of the work week are set in many offices on Monday. You don't want to play catch-up on Tuesday. You'll also miss out on all that meaningless *"How was your weekend?"* crap that no one really cares about but is still critical to fostering professional relationships. I suggest taking Fridays off, or, even better, one of the midweek days. You'll lose the three-day weekend, but you'll never go that long without remaining visible.

Telecommuting

Can you even remember life before e-mail, the Internet, and P.D.A.s? I have a vague recollection of using a typewriter for my first job, but I suspect it's probably just a bad dream. Hard as it is to imagine, there was a time when all that stuff wasn't available to the working masses. Back in the Pleistocene era of the early '90s, if you wanted to communicate with co-workers and business associates, it was the telephone or nothing. *Quel horror!* Today, of course, there are so many ways to stay in touch that you may sometimes wish that you had somewhere to hide.

But all of these technological goodies offer benefits going beyond increased productivity and unsolicited e-mails for mail-order Viagra. More than anything else, they've contributed to the explosion in *telecommuting*, a nifty word for people who do their jobs at home instead of at the office. According to one recent study, over 15 *million* Americans telecommute at least one day a week. With cost-savings to both employer and employee, not to mention social benefits in reducing pollution and traffic congestion, it is likely that telecommuting will only become an increasingly popular alternative work option.

The term "telecommuting" is somewhat misleading. To work properly from home, you'll need more than just a phone. Most telecommuters require at least a fax machine, a separate work area, and fast Internet service to telecommute effectively. Your employer may or may not pick up the costs for these expenses. But even for those who will have to bankroll the home office themselves, the advantages of telecommuting will still likely outweigh these largely one-time expenses. Not to mention the tax write-offs!

For some reason, telecommuting often makes employers more nervous than other work alternatives. Part of it is the old, "How will I know you're not taking tennis lessons or doing laundry?" question. And it's true, some people will abuse the trust and freedom granted to them. But that doesn't mean the whole program should be scrapped. Study after study shows that worker productivity actually *increases* with telecommuters. There are numerous theories for this. Some experts theorize that workers devote part of the time they would spend commuting to work instead. Others believe that freedom from office distractions and politics increases results. I believe the actual reason is more self-serving. As someone who occasionally works from home, I believe most telecommuters treasure the privilege, and happily work overtime to make sure the boss remains satisfied with the arrangement.

If your job lends itself to telecommuting, there are a few things you should know before proposing it to your employer. First, it is *not* a replacement for child care. It's true that you won't have to pay a sitter for time you'd ordinarily spend commuting, but don't think you can negotiate important deals while picking chewing gum out of your kid's hair. A couple I know, both screenwriters, thought they could scrimp on child care for their two kids by working from home. They soon learned that sparkling dialogue and memorable characters don't exactly flow with two screaming children running around. They finally caved and hired a nanny. "We were being penny-wise, pound-foolish," says Glenda. "It was taking us much longer to finish a job, and our writing was suffering. Once we hired someone to come in a few days a week, we could focus without interruption on our work. Working at home is a huge perk, but if you don't go about it the right way, it can be more stressful than any office environment."

Also, don't expect to turn telecommuting into a full-time proposition. Visibility is important, and there will always be meetings and conferences that require face-to-face interaction. Most people telecommute between one and three days per week, or agree to a set number of days per month.

If you have additional questions about telecommuting, or want some advice in the best way to present a proposal to your boss, try www.gilgordon.com. Gordon is a recognized tele-

Not Quite Home Alone: Isabel's Story

When Isabel, an in-house lawyer at a cosmetics firm, was approved to telecommute two days a week, she thought she'd hit the occupational jackpot. She could hold on to her high-paying power job while avoiding the treacherous commute of her congested city. She quickly learned, however, that working from home carries its own unanticipated drawbacks.

"When my kids come home from school, I'm fair game," she says with a laugh. Even with a separate home office, there's no hiding from three inexhaustible boys. To compensate, Isabel schedules the heavy cerebral work and important phone calls in the mornings when she's alone in the house.

Isabel warns other potential telecommuters to be prepared to be on call 24 hours a day. "All boundaries dissolve when you work from home," she notes. The calls and e-mails from headquarters became so constant that Isabel installed a separate business line and began screening her calls in the evenings. Still, she would never consider going back to the office five days a week. To Isabel, organizing the day around three boisterous kids beats being stuck in morning traffic with Howard Stern every morning.

commuting consultant (yes, such a thing actually does exist), and his Website is an excellent comprehensive resource for aspiring telecommuters and the people who employ them.

Division of Labor

Another less common but nonetheless attractive solution for working parents is *job sharing*. With job sharing, you hook up with another person to get the job done. The parties cleave one job down the middle, dividing hours, responsibilities and vacation time between them. Of course, you take home only half your old salary, but your savings in child care expenses mitigate some of that loss. You'll also be able to keep your job skills and Rolodex up to date, so your eventual return to full-time work should go more smoothly.

Many employers instinctively reject this arrangement, though I'm not sure why. Maybe they fear that things will fall through the cracks with two people, or perhaps they worry that both employees will treat the job less seriously. Or it may simply appear too unorthodox to a traditionally-minded boss. To my mind, job sharing is the ultimate win-win situation, provided each person understands and fulfills his share of the job responsibilities.

If this option appeals to you, first find a suitable partner before you present the proposal to your boss. The more concrete information your boss has to help make a decision, the more likely he'll say "yes." Once you've found your partner, tailor your proposal to highlight each of your individual strengths. Don't be shy about pointing out the "two-for-one" benefits to your employer. Without coughing up an extra dime, remind him that he'll double the contacts and have two different minds bringing solutions to the table. Plus, if you've been a dedicated employee all these years, he should know that you're not going to go AWOL any time you're not in the office. Most jobs require you to give beyond 100 percent if you want to get ahead. Job sharing is no different. When you divide your job with another person, the reality is both of you will still work well above your stated 50 percent commitment. When you're a parent, it's easier to go the extra mile when you're not already insanely over-committed at the office.

When Jamie and Brooke, two information technology executives, first proposed a job sharing arrangement to their boss, they met with some resistance. They regrouped, and came up with a deal "sweetener." Instead of working two and a half days a week, each would work three full days, and overlap on Wednesdays. "The extra half day wasn't going to kill either of us, and the company was getting a six-day work week for the price of five," Jamie explains. Their employer rightly figured she was getting a good deal, and quickly approved the new proposal. The arrangement worked beautifully for the three years they worked at the company, and even brought some unforeseen bonuses to all involved. "During the three years we were at the company, neither of us ever took a vacation day or a sick day. Also, each of us felt a responsibility to each other as well as to the company to get the job done. I'd say together we delivered far more than one person ever could have at that job. "

Part-time

Flextime, telecommuting, and job compression all offer ways to modify your schedule without losing a dollar of pay. Though they may keep family life running smoothly, they still require the commitment of a full-time job. Many parents find that even these appealing options stress family life to the breaking point. For these people, a part-time job may be the solution.

The most obvious obstacle to working part-time, of course, is the smaller paycheck you will take home each week. But there are other hurdles to consider as well. Many of us last worked a part-time job in school and, let's face it, probably didn't get rich from it. Most of us associate part-time jobs with polyester uniforms, nametags, and having to ask drunk teens if they want fries with that. And there is some truth to these notions. Most part-time jobs available today offer low pay, minimal benefits, and no career path to speak of. If you're making seven bucks an hour and paying your sitter five, there's not much point, is there?

It *is* possible to find a rewarding part-time job, although you will often have to think outside of the box. One possibility: reduce your current job to part-time status. This may not be the easiest sell to the boss, but there are circumstances (for example, if the company is going through a lean period) where it might actually be welcomed. You will still be on a career track (albeit a slower one), and your salary will be prorated to reflect your reduced hours.

One woman I know came up with a novel solution to working full-time. Wanting to spend more time with her seven-year-old daughter, she dropped out of the rat race and became a part-time teacher at her daughter's private school. Since the school offered free tuition to teachers, the loss of her full-time salary was partially offset by the education savings. Plus, she got to see her daughter more, which was her motive for quitting her job in the first place.

Of course, the right solution will depend on your own unique situation. Be resourceful. You'll almost always end up earning less, but you can make up some of the difference by trimming the fat off your household expenses. Get rid of your cleaning lady, shop at Target, give up the second car if possible. There are very few budgets where money can't be saved. You can wring considerable savings just by eating out less often or skipping a vacation once in awhile. Many people find the trade-off to be well worth it.

Before you begin exploring the world of part-time work, be

prepared to forgo some, if not all, of the benefits full-time workers receive. Most companies provide reduced health coverage and fewer vacation days to part-timers. You probably won't get life insurance either, and your retirement benefits may be affected as well.

THE HAND THAT ROCKS THE CRADLE

Without decent, reliable child care, any work schedule, regardless of how flexible, is doomed to failure. Even non-working mothers must occasionally have access to child care to keep life running on or close to schedule. If you're lucky enough to live next door to Grandma, consider yourself part of a tiny, blessed minority. The rest of us, however, have to turn to outside help—an expensive, frequently scary proposition. No employee is perfect, but nannies have to come pretty damn close. A friend of mine hired a young woman to take care of her infant daughter. The woman seemed like a gift from the heavens for her busy career mom. Conscientious, hardworking, enthusiastic—what more could you ask for in a nanny? One day, however, with the mom at work, the nanny got distracted by a call from her boyfriend. The little girl wandered over to the radiator, stuck her hand on a hot pipe, and received second degree burns!

Of course, the safety of your child should be your primary concern, but for most families the cost of child care runs a close second. Child care is almost always the biggest expense for new working parents. For most people, there is no ideal solution: 24/7 expert child care is simply beyond the limits of most family budgets. There are, however, a range of options available to new families. Juggle the math a little, and you'll probably find one that works for you.

Domestic Horror Story or Comeback Role for Valerie Bertinelli? You Decide.

Seemingly everyone knows someone with a ripped-from-the-headlines horror story involving child care. Oftentimes, good instincts are enough to keep bad news at bay. But not always. A few years ago, a Manhattan nanny accused a professional divorced mom of abusing her two sons. The nanny's credentials were impeccable. She had years of experience and had even written a guide for finding the perfect nanny. The mom, naturally, fell under immediate suspicion and was separated from her kids during the investigation. But a little digging into the nanny's past turned up some interesting revelations. Turns out the nanny had a history of falsely accusing employers as well as her own family members of sexual abuse. The story has a happy ending—the mother got her kids back and the discredited nanny left town—but a more careful reference check could have avoided the whole unpleasant ordeal. (There is—*surprise, surprise*—a Lifetime television movie about the ordeal on the way.)

In-home Care

If you can't be with your child all the time, many parents consider in-home care the next best thing. Your child gets to stay home in a familiar setting and Mommy and Daddy don't have to worry about being greeted by a screaming child if they're running late to the day care center. This is all true, but in-home care comes not without a few trade-offs. For one thing, you'll pay a lot more for the privilege. Secondly, depending on the type of person you hire, you may end up with someone less qualified than the professionals found in day care centers. Lastly, your family will lose some of its treasured privacy. With a full-time live-in, you probably won't be as comfortable sitting around the house in your underwear.

There are two main types of live-in help, *au pairs* and nannies.

Au Pairs Many people confuse *au pairs* with nannies, but the duties of the two are very different. It is important that you understand the difference between them before deciding which best suits your needs.

Au pairs (roughly translated to "as an equal") are European women between the ages of 18 and 25 who want to visit the United States for a year. In exchange for room, board, and a small salary, she agrees to care for your children. The *au pair* program was originally a federal government exchange program that is now overseen by the U.S. State Department.

While most *au pairs* lack the training and experience of their nanny counterparts, they are still required to complete instruction in child safety and development. Your *au pair* should arrive proficient in CPR and other critical skills.

The primary advantage of an *au pair* over a nanny is financial. The U.S. State Department estimates that an *au pair* costs an average of $13,000 a year, substantially less than a nanny. Of course, there are other intangible benefits—your kids will gain early exposure to a foreign culture, an important consideration in these global times.

The biggest drawback to using an *au pair* is the visa restriction on the length of her stay. By law, she can only stay in the U.S. for one year. That means you have to repeat the whole search process after twelve months. Additionally, there are certain living conditions that must be met as well as limits to the number of hours she can work. For more information, go to the U.S. State Department Website, www. state.gov.

There are many agencies that specialize in helping you find an *au pair*. Here are some of the most established:

- Au Pair Programme USA 1-801-255-7722
- Au Pair Homestay USA 1-800-479-0907
- Au Pair Care 1-800-4-AUPAIR
- Au Pair in America 1-800-928-7247
- EurAuPair 1-800-713-2002
- USIA's Exchange Visitor Program Service (202) 401-9810

Nannies If you think you can just place an ad for a nanny and have 100 latter-day Mary Poppinses show up at your doorstep, think again. Today's nannies come from all walks of life, with varying degrees of education and experience. You may still get an *über*-nanny, but today she's much more likely to have a Caribbean lilt than a British accent.

She also won't come cheap. A full-time nanny will cost you about $21,000 a year, plus room and board. If you live in an expensive city, expect to pay more. For many new families, that figure is a deal breaker. If you *can* afford it, many parents swear it's the best way to go. You get dependable care by someone more seasoned than a typical *au pair*. Your kids won't have to say a tearful good-bye every year as they must with an *au pair*. With a little luck (and a nice holiday bonus), she'll stay with your family for years and years.

There's an additional cost to consider when deciding whether to hire a nanny: taxes. Your nanny is your employee, which means her wages are subject to the same Social Security, Medicare, unemployment taxes, etc. that you see on your own pay stub. I'm not going to lie to you—many parents try to evade these taxes by paying their nanny off the books. Most of them get away with it. But some don't, and the IRS is beginning to crack down on the evaders. Get caught and you'll be hit with a heavy fine, and you will never be eligible to run for higher office. These additional taxes will add about 10 to 15 percent to your nanny bill, depending on the state you live in and your arrangement with her. (Many nannies expect you to pick up their part of the FICA contribution.) If it's any consolation, you'll probably qualify for a tax credit for child care, so you'll save some money there.

Day Care

Besides the cost factor, in-home care may not be right for everyone. Your family may not have the living space to accommodate another person, or you simply may not be comfortable surrendering any degree of your family's privacy. Some parents want their children to experience early group socialization, which can be difficult with an in-home nanny.

There are two main choices for out-of-home child care. Regardless of which one appeals to you, both offer substantial savings over private child care.

Family Day Care If you want to keep your child in a familiar domestic environment, family day care may be right for you. In this arrangement, a caregiver watches your child and others in her own home. If she has a large enough group of children, she may (or at least *should*) have someone assisting her.

The hours are often more flexible and it is often easier to find someone willing to take your very young infant. Family day care is especially appealing to parents with children who are easily intimidated by large groups. Most family day care homes accept no more than five or six kids at any one time.

One downside of family day care is a relative lack of regulation. Although many states require certification for family day care operators, some do not. Even in those that do, of course, compliance is never a given. Like most other things, the cost of family day care will vary widely depending on where you live.

If the caregiver is licensed, you'll probably pay more. I shouldn't have to tell you to pay the extra fee—this is one area where cost shouldn't be the deciding factor. Very roughly, expect to pay about $60 to $140 a week.

Incidentally, if you have an abundance of space, patience, and entrepreneurial ambition, you might consider starting a family day care business of your own. Many of these operations are started by parents seeking novel solutions to their own child care problems. Family day care enables them to tend to their own children full-time, while still making money.

Group Day Care Think of group day care as a super-sized version of family day care: more toys, more staff, more play areas, and a lot more kids. Group day care is virtually never run out of a house. With many centers enrolling up to 75 kids, it's not hard to understand why!

Group day care centers may be run by an individual, a chain, a religious organization, or possibly even your local government. Unlike family day care, all fifty states regulate group day care centers, although minimum standards do vary from state to state. Even among regulated centers, quality may vary widely. To help you choose a good center, see the checklist on page 61.

Many parents take comfort in the higher standards centers are held to. The staff will usually have more formal training than a family day care operator, although this does not necessarily translate to better care. You can expect to pay 30 to 50 percent more for group day care than you would for family child care.

Child Care Aware, a program of N.A.C.C.R.A., connects families to local child care experts who can help families locate licensed child care centers. Go to www.childcareaware.org and click the "Child care connector" function.

Child Care Aware suggests using the following guidelines when evaluating a potential care center.

Caregivers/Teachers

- ____ Do the caregivers/teachers seem to really like children?
- ____ Do the caregivers/teachers get down on each child's level to speak to the child?
- ____ Are children greeted when they arrive?
- ____ Are children's needs quickly met even when things get busy?
- ____ Are the caregivers/teachers trained in CPR, first aid, and early childhood education?
- ____ Are the caregivers/teachers involved in continuing education programs?
- ____ Does the program keep up with children's changing interests?
- ____ Will the caregivers/teachers always be ready to answer your questions?
- ____ Will the caregivers/teachers tell you what your child is doing every day?
- ____ Are parents' ideas welcomed? Are there ways for you to get involved?
- ____ Do the caregivers/teachers and children enjoy being together?
- ____ Is there enough staff to serve the children? (Ask local experts about the best staff/child ratios for different age groups.)
- ____ Are caregivers/teachers trained and experienced?
- ____ Have they participated in early childhood development classes?

Setting

- ____ Is the atmosphere bright and pleasant?
- ____ Is there a fenced-in outdoor play area with a variety

of safe equipment? Can the caregivers/teachers see the entire playground at all times?

____ Are there different areas for resting, quiet play, and active play? Is there enough space for the children in all of these areas?

Activities

____ Is there a daily balance of play time, story time, activity time, and nap time?
____ Are the activities right for each age group?
____ Are there enough toys and learning materials for the number of children?
____ Are toys clean, safe, and within reach of the children?

In General

____ Do you agree with the discipline practices?
____ Do you hear the sounds of happy children?
____ Are children comforted when needed?
____ Is the program licensed or regulated?
____ Are surprise visits by parents encouraged?
____ Will your child be happy there?

We Don't Need No Education

It's hard to look at that little gurgling person in the crib and imagine the day 17 years from now when you pack her bags and drop her off on campus. It seems so far away, but freshman orientation week will be here sooner than you think. And with tuition at many private universities now surpassing $25,000 a year, you may not want to think about it at all.

Yes, a college education is expensive, but in today's world, it's more important than ever. This is not about snobbery or having a cool sticker to put on your car's rear window. This is about giving your kids the tools they'll need to compete in tomorrow's world. The chart below shows the median salaries in 2001 for those with different levels of education.

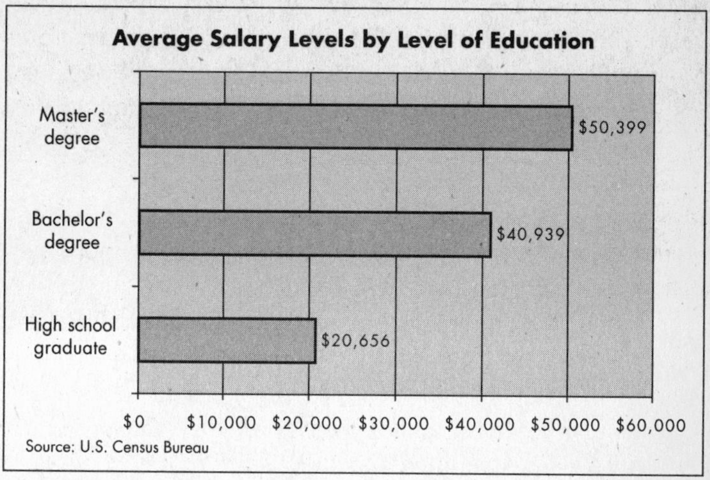

With that gap growing wider by the year, helping your kid attain a college education is no longer a luxury. It's your responsibility. That doesn't mean that you have to pick up the tab for spring break in Bermuda and summers backpacking through Europe. But with the costs of even public universities out of reach for the typical 17-year-old, you'll save a lot of grief later by starting a college savings fund plan today. My own parents didn't anticipate the cost of my college education and saved nothing for it. You can imagine some of the angry arguments we had around the table come application time. Senior year is stressful enough without having to devise ways to get "creative" on the financial aid forms.

The good news is, parents today have attractive savings plans to help meet the rising cost of college: the 529 plan (after the tax code that created it) and the Coverdell account.

The 529 Plans

Two million parents can't be wrong, right? That's how many people have opened 529 plans just in the last two and a half years. Drawn by substantial federal tax breaks, significant improvements in the plans themselves, and increased investment options, many parents have decided that 529 plans are the way to go.

So what are they? 529 plans are investment vehicles that allow you to invest money tax-deferred, provided you use the money to pay for college costs. If you have an IRA, it may help to think of a 529 plan as an IRA for college. In some ways, however, the tax benefits are even better. With a traditional IRA the money is taxed once you start withdrawing the money at retirement. With a 529 plan, however, you get to withdraw the money tax-free. This is a tremendous benefit—a double-whammy in tax saving. The bad news is that this delicious little perk is set to expire in 2010. After that, the earnings on all withdrawals will be subject to taxation. If your child is very young, take heart. With the growing popularity of these plans, there's a reasonable chance Congress may extend the 2010 deadline.

There are two types of 529 plans: prepaid programs and savings programs. Prepaid programs enable you to pay in-state tuition in advance. If your child chooses to attend a private college or an out-of-state public university, you can still apply the money to that school's tuition. (However, you may be penalized, depending on the individual state's policy.) Savings plans offer greater flexibility. You can use the money at any accredited school, which pretty much means anywhere except Bob Jones University.

Many people worry that they will lose out on valuable financial aid if a college sees that they've got a lot of money sitting in a 529 plan. While it's true that your financial aid package will probably be somewhat lower, the total would be even more adversely affected if the money were in your child's name. If the account is in your name, you are expected to contribute only 5.6 percent or less of the account's value for each academic year. Compare that to the 35 percent the university would earmark if the money were instead in a custodial account or in your child's name. Plus, when you consider that financial aid is moving away from grants in favor of loans, the size of the package matters less than you probably think.

Like any government-administered program, the regulations governing 529 plans are complex. Each state operates its own 529 plan, and each has its own rules. (Many states allow you to invest in their plan even if you're not a resident, so it pays to shop around.) If you're serious about starting a 529 plan, I strongly suggest checking out Joseph Hurley's www.savingforcollege.com, an excellent resource that explains different college savings options. Many of the answers to your questions can be found right online, though you can find even more detailed information by investing in Hurley's book, *The Best Way to Save for College—A Complete Guide to 529 Plans.*

Coverdell Accounts

Before 529 plans, the college savings vehicle of choice was the Coverdell account, also known as an educational I.R.A. In light of the advantages of the 529 plan, Coverdell now looks more like a poor cousin. The new plans beat Coverdell accounts in almost every way, save one: you can also use your Coverdell account to pay for your child's private education from grades K through 12. The money in a 529 plan can be used only for college and graduate school.

At the same time, Coverdells have many drawbacks. Currently, you can contribute only a maximum of $2,000 per year to a Coverdell. Your child will probably need much more than that by the time he's ready for college. Compare that to the $250,000 many 529 plans allow you to contribute, and you begin to understand why most parents today prefer 529s.

With a Coverdell, you are merely the custodian of the account. The money actually belongs to your child. That's an important distinction from a 529, where you always retain complete control of the account. While it's not like your child can drain his Coverdell by taking his girlfriend to Hawaii on his 16th birthday, you do surrender some degree of control. Also, since the money is considered your child's asset and not yours, depending on your family's circumstances, he might qualify for less financial aid.

Still, if you are planning to enroll your child in private school, you should consider the Coverdell. You can enroll in one wherever IRAs are sold. (See Chapter 8 for details.)

Though it may seem you can't possibly squeeze another dollar from your family's budget, starting one of these plans early is the best strategy for investing in your child's future. Recent national studies suggest that it is difficult for children in the United States to do better economically than their parents. The figures reveal the correlation between parental and child income:

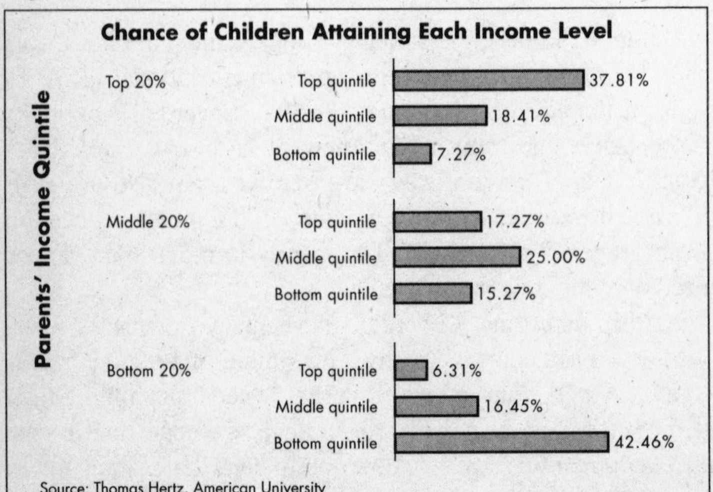

Source: Thomas Hertz, American University

For parents who dream of a better life for their children, the odds are stacked against them. How bad is it? One study found more economic mobility in Sweden than in the U.S. *Sweden!* Land of socialism and universal health insurance!

I wish I was optimistic that these trends would reverse in the future, but all signs point to even rougher sledding ahead for all but the very rich. Between the proposed repeal of the estate tax and massive tax cuts that overwhelmingly flow to the wealthiest 1 percent, it's fair to say that increasing economic opportunity is not a big priority for the current administration. Providing your kid the education he deserves is the best tool you can give him to help him get ahead.

FEARLESS FACTOR

- *Sometimes even "quality time" isn't enough.* Think beyond 9-to-5. Today's employers are more flexible than ever in accommodating the schedules of busy parents. You have a number of options, but how you present the proposal to your boss can often be the determining factor in whether he agrees to an alternative work schedule for you.

- *Child care is usually the biggest expense new parents face.* There are numerous choices for selecting a child care provider, and the costs of each vary significantly. In-home care costs more, but day care offers certain benefits (such as early socialization) that a nanny or *au pair* can't.

- *Education is expensive—and rising!* The gap between the haves and have-nots is widening by the year. The best way to make sure your kid becomes a "have" is to give her the best education you can afford. 529 plans and Coverdell accounts offer major tax breaks that make it easier to save for college.

4

To Buy or Not to Buy: That Is the $235,700* Question

Last summer I visited a friend in L.A. whom I've known since college. Even though she abandoned me for the left coast long ago, we've remained close. The afternoon I arrived we took her dog for a walk through her neighborhood. I hadn't seen my friend in six months, so we had tons to talk about. But instead of catching up on each other's lives, we spent the entire day ogling the houses in her gentrifying neighborhood. Each time we saw a "For Sale" sign, we would marvel at the asking price. This went on for *hours*.

You know you've hit your thirties when you think about real estate so often it becomes almost kinky. You can track someone's age by their obsessions. 21 and under: sex (duh . . .). 22 to 25: it's all about the job. 26 to 29: home furnishings and thread counts. But once we hit 30? It's about square footage, shelter magazines and coveting thy neighbor's condo. I know more than one person who spends his days dodging the boss while surfing real estate listings online. We've all read stories about people getting fired for looking at dirty websites on company time.

* Average sale price of a house in the United States, October 2002.

That's not the real addiction. I bet you'd catch more workers salivating over a 2BR/WBFP with a "motivated seller" than another shot of Jenna Jameson.

Owning a home is no longer the American Dream. It's the American Birthright. A full 68 percent of U.S. households own their own home now. Renters are the new minority. This is less true in other Western countries where the percentage of home ownership is much lower. As any renter knows, however, buying a home is not easy. For a multitude of reasons, our parents (and their parents, for that matter) had an easier time buying a house than we do. Now, with housing prices escalating to infinity and beyond, you may understandably feel doomed to a lifetime of sending checks to your landlord. You shouldn't. Provided you have reasonable expectations (meaning you're okay with the fact that your first house probably won't have a three-car garage and a cottage out back for the maid), there's no reason you too can't own your half-acre slice of suburban bliss.

But First—
Are You Ready to Take the Plunge?

After having a child, buying a house is perhaps the most crucial milestone on the road to full-fledged adulthood. But just as there are plenty of people who reproduce before they're truly ready, there are many others who should think twice before taking on 4,000 square feet of responsibility.

Here are just a few of the things you should consider before you start scouring the classifieds:

- **Your job situation.** Does the future look bright where you work, even for the short term? After writing a check for the down payment and myriad other expenses, many people find they have about $1.92 left in their savings account. You don't want to be in the position of scraping together unemployment checks to cover a brand-new mortgage. I know somebody who had to do just that, and she had to go on medication to cope with the anxiety. I'm not kidding.

- **Your career goals.** Do you get that pit in your stomach every Sunday night at the thought of the week ahead? If so, you're hardly alone. Like an occupational seven-year itch, this is about the age many of us begin to feel restless and contemplate making a major career change. If you're thinking of doing something else with your life, this is probably not the ideal time to buy a house. Changing careers often involves a considerable pay cut until you get some experience. Adjusting to life on a smaller paycheck is hard enough; you don't need to worry about all those new housing expenses as well.

  The same applies double if you need additional schooling for a career change. Even if you're only *thinking* of going back to school, hold off on the house until you decide. Owning a home has its own rewards, but freedom is not one of them. You don't want to narrow your choices either geographically or economically, which is exactly what a hefty mortgage will do to you. Your education comes first. Don't let your shelter fantasies get in the way of investing in yourself.

- **You're one of the chosen people.** If you have a below-market rental, you've already hit the renter's jackpot. As friends bitch and moan about avaricious landlords and double-digit rent increases, you can quietly offer silent thanks to the merciful God of Real Estate. Nothing provokes uncontrollable envy and hatred like a casual mention of your $400 per month loft with skyline views.

  Buying may not be the smartest option if you're already renting the house of your dreams. A friend of mine pays

$900 for a rent-controlled 3 bedroom/2 bathroom apartment in a prime Manhattan neighborhood. That same place would sell for over $1 million on the open market. Her mortgage alone would be over $5,000 a month. Do you think she's going anywhere?

For most people, their home is their biggest asset. If you plan to hold onto your great rental deal, it is critical that you not squander the money you save on your cheap rent. Funnel your savings into alternative investments. Or, if you still really want to invest in real estate, pervert the original egalitarian purpose of rent control and buy a vacation home for you and your lucky family. Don't forget to invite whatever friends you have left.

- **Your relationship.** Being part of a loving, nurturing relationship is one of life's great pleasures. The feeling of waking up next to your beloved, looking across the bed, and wondering how you could ever live without him or her. There's nothing else like it. And then there are those other mornings where you wake up, look across the bed, and wonder how that pillow would look stuffed down his f—ing throat.

  Most relationships have their ups and downs. Before you and your loved one commit to buying a house together, take some time to assess the state of your union. Like children, a house will rarely hold a wobbly relationship together. It will only make the split that much more complicated.

  Exhibit A: A gay couple I know met, fell in love, and quickly decided to move in together. (Hold the lesbian U-Haul jokes. The couple in this story are two men.) They lived in a rapidly gentrifying neighborhood. Sensing a terrific investment, they pooled their money and bought a large loft together. The value of the loft skyrocketed. Unfortunately, their relationship crashed. Now, in a kind of same-sex *War of the Roses*, each refuses to leave. Neither will sell his share to the other. The break-up was *two years ago*. I don't care how much money is at stake. Who wants to live in an environment where "Honey, I'm home" is a warning, not a greeting?

- **Terrorism.** On a more somber note, any discussion of real estate (or at least any discussion of urban real estate) must acknowledge the increased risks of domestic terrorism. I hesitated before including this, but after listening to friends of mine who own homes in high-risk areas, I decided I had to. Not discussing it would be like ignoring the proverbial 800-pound gorilla in the room. He's still there, even if you're closing your eyes.

  I live in New York. Immediately after 9/11, most people I know were determined not to let the actions of a few deranged extremists control their lives. Now, however, as the threat of terrorism shows no sign of abating, I've noticed a slow but measurable softening of that stance. Friends who previously swore "not to let them win" now openly wonder what they would do if their city was hit by another terrorist attack.

  One couple I know bought a beautiful apartment just two months before 9/11. Unfortunately, the excitement of owning their first home is now seriously tempered by the constant anxiety that their biggest asset is vulnerable to the unthinkable. After months of a painstaking renovation, they are seriously contemplating selling their house and moving away from the city. "For us, it's less an issue of physical safety than it is about avoiding financial devastation. The issue isn't surviving a terrorist attack. The odds of being in the wrong place at the wrong time are still quite small. We'll take that risk. But can the psychology of the city withstand another attack? I'm not sure. And, God forbid if there's a so-called dirty bomb and whole neighborhoods become uninhabitable. There's no insurance plan on earth that will protect a city from that. We'd be wiped out."

I'm not suggesting that anyone live a life dictated by fear, but it is completely valid to weigh the additional risk of terrorism in deciding when and where to buy.

How Much House Can You Afford?

So, you've taken a long look at your personal situation, assessed your finances, and decided that yes, you want that room of your own. You've taken an important psychological step toward signing on the dotted line. Now, however, you need to focus on the practical—how much can you realistically put forth to buy and maintain a house without driving yourself crazy with anxiety?

Many a thirtysomething has set himself up for a crash by letting big house dreams get ahead of realistic budgets. Why spend your weekends looking at houses fit for a millionaire if you won't even qualify for a Home Depot credit card after making the down payment? Perhaps you've heard the expression "house-poor" before. Basically, that's when a couple moves into a beautiful new house and sits on the floor in the dark eating ramen noodles each night because they can't afford meat, electricity, or a sofa to sit on. Enjoying your house becomes virtually impossible when you spend every free minute sweating over the bills. I know a guy who spent a year building his dream house on prime California beachfront. Several million dollars later, he moved in, only to discover he couldn't afford the upkeep. (He works in a highly cyclical profession.) Three years after settling in, he put the house on the market.

Most personal finance experts advise you to spend no more than 28 percent of your monthly gross income on a mortgage payment. This is a fast-and-loose number that should be used only as a general guideline. Your budget may be able to accommodate a greater or lower percentage, depending on your own individual circumstances. A childless couple, for example, will likely have fewer monthly expenses than a family with four little mouths to feed. Also, if you are in a profession that offers substantial pay hikes or bonuses, you may be able to push the borrowing limits a little higher knowing that you will have more income in the near future. If you do stick to the 28 percent rule, the chart below shows a range of salaries and the maximum annual and monthly mortgage payments you should consider. (Remember, too, that there are four and a half weeks in a month. Many people forget this and simply multiply their weekly paycheck by four. Strangely, banks seem to have no problem lending hundreds of thousands of dollars to people who don't know there are 31 days in some months.)

The 28 Percent Rule

If Your Salary Is . . .	*Your Monthly Mortgage Payment Should Not Exceed . . .*
$25,000	$583.33
35,000	816.67
45,000	1,040.00
55,000	1,283.33
65,000	1,516.67
75,000	1,750.00
85,000	1,983.33
95,000	2,216.67
105,000	2,450.00

City Slicker Sticker Shock

If you live in a high-priced city such as San Francisco or Boston, you can count on forking over far more than 28 percent of your salary to your mortgage lender each month. Banks understand this, and, depending on your credit situation, many will approve mortgages of up to 40 percent of your monthly gross income. While that number should give anyone pause, good public transportation systems (making a car and costly car insurance unnecessary) and frequently lower real estate taxes can help mitigate the extra mortgage bite.

THE KEY TO THE KINGDOM: THE DOWN PAYMENT

For many first-time homebuyers, coming up with that initial down payment seems like a cruel joke. Says one despondent thirty-year-old I know: "I live in Manhattan, where decent one-bedrooms start at $400,000. Here, you need 20 percent to get a mortgage. Who has $80,000 sitting around? It's getting so bad in this city. I don't know anyone who's bought an apartment without parental assistance. One professional forty-year-old woman I know just bought her first apartment. She had to ask her mother for help! You begin to believe the system is out to get you. At the rate I'm going, I'll have a down payment when I'm fifty!"

To be fair, Manhattan is a cruel mistress, merciless and unforgiving. But with housing prices climbing nationwide, the thirty-year-old above has lots of frustrated company. Average home prices in many major metropolitan areas experienced single and double-digit price gains throughout the past decade. The nineties have been very good for those who got in early.

For those who are still renting, buying a first home has admittedly gotten a bit more challenging.

If you're far from having enough cash for a down payment, don't despair. There are still many options available to you:

- **Save, stupid.** "Yeah, great, thanks," you're probably saying. "Like I haven't tried that already." But saving in your thirties is a different experience than trying to save money in your twenties. Chances are you're making more money, your student loans are gone, you've hopefully winnowed down the credit card debt. If this describes you, then you will probably find you can amass a healthy down payment far sooner than you thought possible. Make your down payment your number one priority. Figure out how much you'll need and earmark a percentage of your weekly paycheck for your down payment. If you can bank $150 a week for three years, you'll have $23,400!
- **Borrow from your 401(k) plan.** It's your money, right? Why not put it to use now? Most companies allow you to borrow from your 401(k) plan for a first-time home purchase. (Maybe they figure an employee who's put down roots is more likely to stay with the company.) When you signed up for your 401(k) plan, you were probably advised of the severe penalties for making withdrawals. But *borrowing* from your 401(k) plan (which means, yes, you do have to pay the money back) is often permissible. There are limits, so check with Human Resources for your company's policy. One caveat: since you must repay the plan, lenders will consider the amount you borrow as part of your overall debt when computing your debt-to-income ratio. If you have other substantial debt obligations, it may make it more difficult to qualify for a mortgage.
- **Put down a smaller down payment.** Yes, it's possible to find a lender who will take a chance on you if your other

vitals (credit history, income) look solid. There are still lenders out there who will grant you a mortgage with as little as 3 percent down.

Not surprisingly, this option comes with a number of downsides. One, since you are borrowing more, your monthly payment will naturally be higher. Two, more mortgage = more interest, and interest is already a major part of your total mortgage expense in the most optimum of circumstances. Finally, you will be required to purchase something called private mortgage insurance (or PMI), which protects your lender should you default.

- **Investigate your state's mortgage program.** What if I told you there's an institution that offers low-interest, low-down payment mortgages that you can get without ever stepping foot into a bank? And no, I'm not referring to those cheesy late-night infomercials with guys throwing money at the screen. *("No credit! No problem!")* I'm talking about your own state government. As a first-time home buyer there's a program available for you, no matter where in the fifty states you live.

  Naturally, this being the government, there are a jumble of restrictions. Also, since this is not a federal program, each state can make up its own list of eligibility requirements. Generally speaking, however, most states require that your household income be less than the state or county average and the cost of the house you want to buy be below the average cost of homes in your area. Check with your own state's agency for their specific policies. The list on page 81 provides Web addresses and phone numbers for all state housing agencies.

- **Give your Aunt Fannie and Uncle Freddie a call.** With these two programs, you can no longer ask what the U.S. government has ever done for you. There are a few differences between the Federal National Mortgage Association

All About PMI

The annual cost of private mortgage insurance is calculated by multiplying the mortgage by a percentage, usually .05 percent. A $200,000 house minus a 10 percent down payment (or $20,000) would require insurance coverage on the $180,000 loan. You could reasonably expect to pay about $900 per year for private mortgage insurance. ($180,000 x .05 percent).

This additional expense may seem annoying, particularly if you have an excellent credit history. You can take comfort in knowing it's not forever. Most lenders let you drop PMI once you've reached 20 percent equity in your home. Even better, once you reach 22 percent equity, PMI is automatically dropped, *and* you may even be entitled to a partial refund. For more information, visit the Department of Housing and Urban Development's Website at www.hud.gov. Or you can try calling them at (202) 708-1113. This being a government agency, by the time you get off "hold," you might have already paid off your mortgage!

Depending on your situation, you may be able to avoid PMI by obtaining a second mortgage. This is a fairly tricky proposition, so you'll probably need the services of a savvy mortgage broker (see end of chapter). Going this route can save you money in two ways: most of the time, it is cheaper monthly, and the interest on the second mortgage is tax-deductible, whereas PMI is not.

(Fannie Mae) and the Federal Home Loan Mortgage Corporation (Freddie Mac). Both, however, offer terrific mortgage plans for the *in-betweeners*—people who earn too much money to qualify for a state mortgage but can't meet the requirements for a traditional one either.

Requirements for eligibility are substantially softer than a traditional bank mortgage. Freddie requires only a 5 percent down payment to qualify for a mortgage. Fannie is even more lax, requiring only 3 percent down. With some exceptions, there are no income ceilings, although there is a maximum amount you can borrow. The amount changes yearly, so it's best to check with the programs for the most current limits. (For 2003, the limit for both programs is $322,700.) Also, unlike a state housing agency mortgage, interest rates are comparable to a traditional mortgage. Still, if you don't qualify for a state mortgage, this may be the way to go. Check out www.freddiemac.com and www.fanniemae.com for full details.

- **Or, try Freddie and Fannie's love child, the FHA.** Say your credit history is less than perfect. You could set your clock to the nightly calls from American Express, you just "couldn't deal" with those student loan payments in your twenties, blah blah blah. Believe it or not, you are not doomed to a lifetime of rapacious landlords and living below Metallica wanna-bees. The Federal Housing Administration just might be your savior.

  The FHA does not offer mortgages directly to the borrower. Rather, it offers insurance to the financial institution underwriting your mortgage. Should you default, the bank suffers no loss. It simply turns to the FHA and says, "Pay up!" (Which doesn't mean you're off the hook, of course. The FHA will then come after you.) With the U.S. government backing up your mortgage, a lender can take a bigger risk on you than it would otherwise. With an FHA mortgage, you're only required to put down a small down payment—between 3 percent and 5 percent.

These loans offer a great opportunity for people who might otherwise be shut out of owning their own home, but they do come with a few caveats. If you put down a lower down payment, your monthly payment will naturally be higher. The government doesn't pick up the tab for the insurance, so you will also have that additional burden to shoulder. (It also costs a bit more than private mortgage insurance.)

There are limits to the amount you can borrow, and if you live in a city with out-of-control housing prices, you may very well come up short. For example, the current loan limit for San Francisco is $280,749. The average price of a house in San Francisco in 2002 was $537,000. Happy hunting!

Telephone Numbers and Web Addresses for State Housing Agencies

	Telephone Number	Website
Alabama	(334) 244-9200	www.ahfa.com
Alaska	(907) 338-6100	www.ahfc.state.ak.us
Arizona	(602) 280-1365	www.housingaz.com
Arkansas	(501) 682-5900	www.accessarkansas.org/adfa
California	(916) 322-3991	www.caohfa.ca.gov
Colorado	(303) 297-2432	www.colohfa.org
Connecticut	(860) 721-9501	www.chfa.org
Delaware	(302) 739-4263	www2.state.de.us/dsha
Florida	(850) 488-4197	www.floridahousing.org
Georgia	(404) 679-4840	www.dca.state.ga.us
Hawaii	(808) 587-0567	www.hcdch.state.hi.us
Idaho	(208) 331-4883	www.ihfa.org
Illinois	(312) 836-5200	www.ihda.org
Indiana	(317) 232-7777	www.indianahousing.org
Iowa	(515) 242-4990	www.ifahome.com
Kansas	(785) 296-5865	www.kansascommerce.com
Kentucky	(502) 564-7630	www.kyhousing.org
Louisiana	(225) 763-8700	www. lhfa.state.la.us
Maine	(207) 626-4600	www.mainehousing.org
Maryland	(410) 514-7400	www.dhcd.state.md.us
Massachusetts	(617) 854-1020	www.masshousing.com
Michigan	(517) 373-8370	www.michigan.gov/mshda
Minnesota	(651) 296-7608	www.mhfa.state.mn.us
Mississippi	(601) 718-4612	www.mshc.com
Missouri	(816) 759-6600	www.mhdc.com

	Telephone Number	Website
Montana	(406) 841-2840	www.commerce.state.mt.us/housing
Nebraska	(402) 434-3900	www.nisa.org
Nevada	(702) 486-7220	www.nvhousing.state.nv.us
New Hampshire	(603) 472-8623	www.nhhfa.org
New Jersey	(800) 654-6873	www.nj-hmfa.com
New Mexico	(505) 843-6880	www.housingnm.org
New York	(800) 382-4663	www.nyhomes.org
North Carolina	(919) 877-5700	www.nchfa.com
North Dakota	(701) 328-8080	www.ndhfa.org
Ohio	(614) 466-7970	www.odod.state.oh.us/ohfa
Oklahoma	(405) 848-1144	www.ohfa.org
Oregon	(503) 986-2015	www.hcs.state.or.us
Pennsylvania	(717) 780-3800	www.phfa.org
Rhode Island	(401) 751-5566	www.rihousing.com
South Carolina	(803) 734-2000	www.sha.state.sc.us
South Dakota	(605) 773-3181	www.sdhda.org
Tennessee	(615) 741-4968	www.state.tn.us/thda
Texas	(512) 475-2120	www.tdhca.state.tx.us
Utah	(801) 521-6950	www.utahhousingcorp.org
Vermont	(802) 864-5743	www.vhfa.org
Virginia	(804) 782-1986	www.vhda.com
Washington	(206) 464-7139	www.wshfc.org
Washington, D.C.	(202) 408-0415	www.dchfa.org
West Virginia	(304) 345-6475	www.wvhdf.com
Wyoming	(307) 265-0603	www.wyomingcda.com

Tax Scratch Fever

Once you start making a decent salary, your accountant will probably give you the inevitable lecture about the tax advantages of owning your own home. (Or maybe that's just my accountant, who doles out so much advice each tax season he must have been a Jewish mother in a previous life.) While it's true that a house can fatten your tax refund, you must understand exactly how your tax situation will change before you buy. Both the money you give to—and get back from—the government changes dramatically once you transition from renter to owner. Knowing what to expect each April 15 will make your life as a new homeowner much less stressful.

Property Taxes

If you've ever looked through the real estate classifieds, you've noticed that after all those lovely descriptions of "4 br/3 bath on 3/4 wooded acres" there often follows a hideously depressing number: the annual property tax. This is the annual tax that you, as a homeowner, must pay to the community the house is located in. The majority of this tax is earmarked for local schools. Speaking broadly, school districts within high-tax communities usually rank higher than those in low-tax districts. If children are in your future, high property taxes will probably pay off for you. There's a definite correlation between high tax communities and kids bound for Harvard, Princeton, and Yale. The property tax rate can be a useful barometer of a community's values as well as an indication of the quality of the schools. This is one instance where, regarding taxation, you usually get what you pay for.

Many people would find high property taxes a deal-breaker when it comes to their ability to buy. The U.S. government lessens the burden by allowing homeowners to deduct the entire property tax bill from their federal tax bill. That's a pretty nice gift from the IRS, an institution typically not known for its generosity.

Say you bought a $275,000 home in suburban Ann Arbor, Michigan, as two friends of mine recently did. They pay about $3,500 in property taxes, not an unreasonable amount for the area. Now, that's a hard number to stomach, especially for a young couple just starting out. But they get to take the $3,500 as a deduction (Line 7 of Schedule A), which considerably lowers their adjustable gross income, or AGI. (The AGI is the amount subject to taxation after all deductions and exemptions are taken. Your goal as a taxpayer is to whittle that number down—*legally*—as low as possible.)

Mortgage Interest

This is the tax deduction motherlode. For the life of your mortgage, the IRS allows you to deduct every dollar of interest from your mortgage. In the example above, my friends put down 20 percent on their house, giving them a $220,000 mortgage. Last year, they paid about $7,200 in mortgage interest. (And you bitched about the interest on your Amex Optima statement . . .) Once again, Schedule A comes to the rescue. Line 10 invites you to deduct the full amount from your AGI.

Case Study

Kristin and Doug are your typical upwardly mobile professional thirtysomething couple. Kristin met Doug in her mid-twenties, when she was in graduate school and he was studying to be a computer engineer. Before they decided to tie the knot, they shared an apartment in Boston. Years later ("Doug takes a while to motivate," jokes Kristin), Doug, now a full-fledged engineer, proposed to Kristin, now working in publishing. Soon after the honeymoon, Doug and Kristin took a hard look at their finances and decided a move to the 'burbs was inevitable. "We wanted to start a family soon, and there was no way I was going to send my child to a Boston public school. Doug and I are both progressive, but I am not willing to jeopardize my child's education to make a political statement. We looked into private schools in the area, but we just couldn't afford tuition. So we really only had one option—find a house in a town with decent public schools."

After a seemingly endless parade of Saturday morning open houses, Doug and Kristin finally found a house they both liked and could afford ("No mean feat," says Kristin) about sixty miles outside of the city. By combining their savings and the money their parents gave them for their wedding, they put down $63,000, or 20 percent, on a $315,000 condominium. While their old rent pales in comparison to their mortgage and property tax bill, Kristin says the move was the smartest thing they've ever done. "Our mortgage comes to about $1,500 a month and we pay about $5,000 a year in property taxes. That's more than we were paying in rent, and in the beginning, having less money in the bank at the end of each month took some getting used to. But now I actually look forward to tax season. Our tax bill is so much lower than when we rented." Kristin estimates that after the tax break is factored in, she and Doug pay only about $200 more than when they were renting. Not bad, especially when you consider, as Kristin says, "We're building equity for ourselves, and not our old, horrible landlord."

Points

At the close of your mortgage, you may be assessed something called points. This is a fee typically between 1 and 3 percent of your total mortgage. (It is often possible to find a zero-point loan, particularly in competitive areas, but many times these loans do not have the lowest interest rates.) Since points are actually nothing more than interest paid in advance, it makes sense that you get to deduct these on your return as well. Even though points are a one-time charge, they sting. On a $200,000 mortgage, you could expect to be charged between $2,000 and $6,000 in points. You can take the deduction all at once or amortize it over the life of the loan.

Capital Gains

If you've ever invested money in the stock market or even deposited money in a low-interest savings account, you know all too well that the IRS makes money when you do. Taxes on so-called capital gains (defined as the profit on an investment) can take a considerable chunk out of your profits, sometimes so much so that you may be left wondering why you bother to invest in the first place.

In the late nineties, the government amended the tax code so that the profits realized from the sale of a house were largely exempt from capital gains taxes. Since for most people their home is their biggest asset, this is a huge windfall for most homeowners. For example, say you sell your house for $100,000 more than you bought it for (entirely possible in today's white-hot housing market). If you made the exact same amount in the stock market, depending on circumstances, you could reasonably expect to fork over about $20,000 in capital gains taxes.

Now, before you rush out and plunk down a fortune for the McMansion of your dreams, there are certain restrictions you need to be aware of. First, there are maximums to the amount you can claim tax-free—$250,000 for singles, $500,000 for couples. Everything after that is fair game for the long reach of the IRS. (Although if you've made that much money on your house, you don't really have much to complain about, do you?) Second, you only get to take full advantage of the law once every two years. This prevents people from flipping houses and speculating. There are also some other conditions of residency the government imposes, though you, as a first-time home buyer, probably don't have to worry about them. The important thing to understand is that, as a homeowner, you get major tax advantages not only on the front end, when you buy, but also on the back end, when it's time to sell.

Fearless Factor

- *Home ownership is the American Dream, but is it right for you?* No one wants to rent forever, but your individual circumstances may favor delaying moving day for a while. Those considering a career change or going back to school might not want the additional stress of a mortgage hanging over their heads.

- *They're called "starter homes" for a reason.* Many first-time buyers' eyes are bigger than their down payments. Don't set yourself up for heartbreak by shooting for a house you can't afford. Even if you can come up with the down payment, the hefty mortgage you carry may prevent you from enjoying the place you live.

- *The U.S. tax code favors homeowners over renters.* When you own a home, you can deduct mortgage interest, property taxes, and points from your tax bill. You are also exempt from capital gains taxes on any profits (up to certain maximums) you realize from the sale of your house.

- *Take advantage of special programs for home buyers.* There are federal and state programs available to first-time home buyers that offer low-interest and/or lowdown payment mortgages. Each state has its own rules, but if you qualify, these programs can save you a bundle.

5

Mortgage Madness

Most first-time home buyers approach the mortgage application process with equal parts fear and dread. Choosing the perfect home is stressful enough, and once you do you've still got some work ahead of you. Now you've got to convince a large, impersonal institution that you're deserving of a loan that could feed a Third World country for a year. Perhaps you've seen that bank commercial where the guy combs through the county dump looking for a missing pay stub he needs for his mortgage application? It's meant to be funny, but for anybody applying for his first mortgage, it can seem frighteningly real.

It needn't be. The process is intimidating in part because of its complete unfamiliarity to most of us. As you will soon see, mortgages come in many different stripes and colors. While initially the choices may seem overwhelming, you should view this diversity as an opportunity to find the perfect mortgage to suit your needs. Familiarizing yourself now with your available options will give you time to focus on what's really important later—like finding that pay stub from 1996.

FIRST THINGS FIRST

Finding the perfect mortgage won't do you any good if you don't have the documents you need to get approved. Most lenders require that you provide the following items. Have them ready upon request.

In a file, keep clean, neat copies of the following:

- W-2 forms for the last two years and two consecutive pay stubs. Self-employed people should provide tax returns from the last three years. If you haven't saved them, *tsk tsk.* You can request copies from your accountant or the IRS.
- Your employer's vitals (name, address and phone number).
- Statements of all financial assets, such as mutual funds, savings bonds, bank accounts, 401(k) statements, etc. covering the most recent three-month period.
- List of all liabilities, such as student loans, credit cards, etc. (Your credit report will reveal these anyway, so no sense trying to hide them.)
- Documentation establishing your place of residence for the last year. (Usually a letter from your landlord is enough, but you can also provide twelve months of cancelled rent checks.)
- If you own at least 25 percent of a company, than you will need the last two years of your corporate tax returns.

You'll note from the list above that a lender is interested in much more than just your assets and income. He will be taking a close look at your debts as well. Your mortgage payment will most likely be your largest monthly expense; a lender wants to be reasonably confident that your existing debts won't interfere with your ability to mail his payment in on time. (Though it may vary somewhat from lender to lender, the general rule of thumb is that your total debt payments, including your mortgage, shouldn't exceed 36 percent of your gross income for loans currently under $322,700. Jumbo Loans above that amount allow the slightly higher debt-to-income ratio of 38 percent.)

Regardless of your credit rating, if you carry a lot of debt, you may find it more difficult to qualify for a mortgage, particularly if your debt knocks you above the debt-to-income threshold. I know people who routinely carry $10,000 on their credit cards. That's a *minimum* monthly payment of about $200. Any prospective lender looking at that number is not likely to be inspired by your fiscal management skills.

Before taking the mortgage plunge, whittle your debts down to a more manageable size. You'll not only be a more appealing loan candidate, you won't feel as strapped come moving day. Or, put another way: once you pay off your cards, there's that much more room to charge them back up at the 24-hour Lowe's near you!

Nice Try

If you think you can borrow a lump sum from your parents or a friend and pay off your plastic a week before you apply for a mortgage, think again. Lenders weren't born yesterday. They scrutinize your payment patterns for up to a year before the application date. If they see that you wiped out your debts with one swift payment, you can bet they will ask where you got the money.

AN EMBARRASSMENT OF (BORROWED) RICHES: WHICH MORTGAGE IS RIGHT FOR YOU?

The mortgage application process requires you to make decisions every step of the way. The two biggest choices you will have to make involve the length of time you want to carry the mortgage and the type of rate plan you are comfortable with.

Fixed-rate Mortgages

If you fear the unknown, this is the mortgage for you. The name says it all: the interest rate you and your lender agree to when you sign up for the mortgage remains constant, or fixed, throughout the life of the mortgage. That means the amount on the first check you send will be the same amount as your last payment. The only thing that changes is the date on the check.

Fixed-rate mortgages are reassuring for obvious reasons. You can see in the table on page 93 how a single-point increase in interest rates can dramatically affect your monthly payment. With a fixed-rate mortgage, you don't have to nervously contemplate where you'll come up with the extra cash should rates spike suddenly. That stability is appealing to many people. Fixed-rate mortgages are by far the most popular type of mortgage.

Although fixed-rate mortgages seem designed for the cautious among us, they are not entirely without risk. What happens if you buy a house when rates are high and rates then drop? You're locked in to a high-rate mortgage as the world around you enjoys lower rates. Yes, you can always refinance your mortgage, but the costs of refinancing may eat up any savings if the rate spread isn't substantial enough.

Adjustable-rate Mortgage

Another imaginatively titled type of mortgage is the adjustable-rate mortgage (or ARM), which is exactly what it sounds like. With an adjustable-rate mortgage, the rate you pay varies, often considerably, over the life of the loan. The rate is usually fixed for a certain period (anywhere from 3, 5, 7, or

10 years) and then adjusted afterward (most commonly every year thereafter). There are many variations in ARM schedules. For example, some mortgages may fix the rate for the first 5 years and then adjust it once for the remaining 25. You have considerable flexibility in choosing the terms of your ARM.

ARMs can be appealing to home buyers for a number of reasons. If interest rates are high when you are shopping for a mortgage, ARMs offer the strong possibility that you'll pay a lower rate in the future. There are often no points to pay with an ARM mortgage, which offers immediate savings to cash-crunched home shoppers. Lastly, the initial interest rate you sign up for can be significantly lower than a fixed-rate mortgage's.

As a holder of an adjustable-rate mortgage, you are not left completely exposed to the vagaries of the open market. You do have some built-in protections. Most ARMs have caps limiting the size of any single interest rate jump, and there is often a maximum interest rate your mortgage can never exceed, no matter how high interest rates may climb over time. Still, a move of just one percentage point can cost you dearly. You must be prepared for that possibility with an ARM.

ARMs are good for people who are reasonably certain they will not be living in their house for a long time. You save money in the short term, and by the time the rate adjusts, you may be on to your next house. However, you should consider an adjustable-rate mortgage only if you are psychologically and financially comfortable with a certain amount of risk, *or* if present interest rates are so high that it is unlikely they will climb much higher.

How Interest Rates Affect Monthly Mortgage Payments
(30-Year Mortgage)

Mortgage Amount	Interest Rate					
	6%	6.5%	7.5%	8%	8.5%	9%
$150,000	$899.33	$948.10	$1048.82	$1100.65	$1153.37	$1206.93
200,000	1199.10	1264.14	1398.43	1467.53	1537.83	1609.25
250,000	1498.88	1580.17	1748.04	1834.41	1922.28	2011.56
300,000	1798.65	1896.20	2097.64	2201.29	2306.74	2413.87
350,000	2098.43	2212.24	2447.25	2568.18	2691.20	2816.18
400,000	2398.20	2528.27	2796.86	2935.06	3075.65	3218.49

One Mortgage That'll Suck the Air Out of Your Finances

Balloon mortgages offer lower monthly payments for a set number of years and then require you to pay off the remaining balance in one lump sum. Sound scary? It is. If that inheritance or mega-bonus doesn't come through as planned, you could easily find yourself in default. Most financial advisers do not recommend balloon mortgages.

You could refinance your mortgage, but if the value of your home has fallen at the time you need a new mortgage, you will have a hard time finding a lender who will underwrite a new one. Most of us prove to be pretty bad at predicting the future with any degree of accuracy. Unless you know with 100 percent absolute certainty that you will have the money to pay off that last huge payment, you should steer clear of this mortgage.

So . . . What Are You Doing for the Next Thirty Years?

It should surprise no one that, given the choice of repaying a six-figure loan over 15 years or 30, the vast majority of mortgage holders prefer to take their own sweet time. By the time most of us are ready to commit to a mortgage, debt has almost become an ingrained part of our DNA. We spend our post-college years swimming in student loans and our late twenties paying off Amex-financed excesses. To not be in some kind of long-term debt seems almost . . . un-American.

While both types of mortgages have their selling points, as a first-time home buyer you might be better off with the comfort zone and flexibility a longer-term mortgage offers.

Though the monthly payments are substantially higher than a 30-year mortgage, 15-year mortgages have one principal advantage, and it's a big one. You will save thousands and thousands of dollars in interest. The chart below shows just how much interest a hypothetical homeowner would save on a $250,000 mortgage:

Total Interest Paid for 15- and 30-Year Mortgages at 7 Percent Interest

	$100,000	$200,000	$300,000	$400,000	$500,000
15-year	$61,788.85	$123,577.70	$185,367.93	$247,156.78	$308,945.33
30-year	139,511.04	279,022.09	418,524.53	558,035.58	697,546.62

Not exactly small potatoes, is it? And, when you consider that the interest rate on a 15-year mortgage is usually slightly lower than its 30-year counterpart, you actually save even more.

So why would anyone who could handle the increased payments of a 15-year mortgage choose to pay all that extra interest that comes with a 30-year mortgage? In a word, taxes. Remember, every dollar of mortgage interest is tax-deductible. With a

15-year-mortgage, a higher portion of your monthly payment goes to building equity in the house. You get a nice feeling of accomplishment, but accomplishments aren't deductible. Many people also prefer to take the money saved from a lower monthly payment a 30-year mortgage offers and invest it instead. If you've snagged a low interest rate and can invest the extra money smartly, this might be an attractive benefit of a longer-term mortgage. It also helps protect you in case of a financial disaster—you have more cash available to live off of over the years, so there is less of a risk that you'll lose your house.

Tales from the Home Front

Annie and Roland, a couple in their early thirties, agree on most things, but when it came time to choosing a 15- or 30-year mortgage for their first home, both dug in their heels. "Roland is much more comfortable with owing money than I am," Annie says with some degree of understatement. "I am almost pathologically opposed to debt." Both make good money, so they could easily handle the larger monthly payment of a 15-year mortgage. Roland, however, didn't want to tie up any more money than absolutely necessary. "My feeling was, we're both young. Who knows what the future will bring? What happens if one of us burns out on the corporate grind and wants to teach underprivileged kids or something? I didn't want us to be handcuffed to our bank for the next fifteen years." Finally, they reached a compromise: Annie told Roland she would agree to a 30-year mortgage if they made a commitment to paying it off early. It wasn't too difficult for Roland to find a 30-year mortgage with no prepayment penalty. And Annie? "I'm not sure Roland knows this, but I'm still planning a mortgage-burning party in 2016!"

Finding the Best Mortgage Lender

In the same way one airline will quote you $200 for a round-trip ticket while another will quote you $350 for the exact same flight, the cost of an identical mortgage can vary considerably from one lender to another. If you want the best deal, you'll have to devote some time to shopping for it. It may be tempting to just go to the bank where you have your checking account or ask a friend where he got his mortgage. Don't. Just because your bank offers no-fee checking doesn't mean their mortgage offerings are a great deal. Banks also adjust their rates all the time. Your friend's lender might have offered the best deal at the time, but that was then and this is now. You have no guarantee that someone else isn't offering better rates today.

Check out the real estate section of your local paper to get a sense of the current range of rates. Many papers will print the rates of specific local and national banks. Others may list the average rates in the region for the different types of mortgages. This is a little less helpful perhaps, but will still allow you to compare a specific lender's rates to what's around. The newspaper will also likely be filled with advertisements from lenders. You should look into these, but exercise due diligence. Often these ads contain little more than the interest rate and a phone number. A low interest rate is great, but be on the lookout for hidden fees and excessive points, which can add thousands of dollars onto the cost of the loan.

And of course, no mortgage hunt would be complete without a spin on the World Wide Web. The Internet has dozens of reputable sites that can help you find a competitive deal. Some of the most widely used are www.hsh.com, www.compareinterestrates.com, and www.lendingtree.com.

Mortgage Brokers

With the Internet and a little elbow grease, there's no reason you can't conduct your own investigation for the best mortgage deal. However, it might make sense to use the services of a mortgage broker. It doesn't cost you anything, and if you're the kind of person who would rather sit through a wall-to-wall marathon of Madonna movies than deal with all that paperwork, a mortgage broker could be your salvation.

Mortgage brokers do the shopping for you. They are paid on commission from mortgage lenders. Usually, a broker's rates will be better than a bank's because they deal with the wholesale mortgage side of the bank. As an individual, you deal with the retail side. Most brokers will have access to the lowest rates out there, but you still have to do your homework. You still may find better rates somewhere else. For example, some banks with low rates don't work with brokers.

Engaging the service of a mortgage broker doesn't mean you must ultimately choose a mortgage from him, so you should check his offerings against the Web to ensure the mortgages he's offering are competitive. If they are, go with him. He'll be an invaluable guide as you wade your way through the application process.

The National Association of Mortgage Planners runs a Website (namp.org) that can provide you with questions to ask a prospective broker and help you locate a broker in your area. (At the time of this writing only a few states are represented.)

Fearless Factor

- *Paper clips and folders—your two best friends in the application process.* Applying for a mortgage can be a dizzying experience. You'll have an easier go of it if you stay calm and organized.

- *Get your own financial house in order before you apply for a mortgage.* Lenders look carefully at your outstanding debts and your credit rating when assessing your application. Check your credit report for errors *before* you apply, and pay down your debts.

- *Mortgages aren't one-size-fits-all.* You can choose a mortgage with a fixed rate, an adjustable rate, a 15-year or a 30-year payment period. Most people go with a 30-year, fixed-rate mortgage, but that may not be right for your circumstances. Investigate the pros and cons of each mortgage type carefully.

- *Consider using a mortgage broker.* They don't cost you anything, and they can help first-time buyers stay on top of the mountain of paperwork lenders require. Just check to make sure he is offering you a competitive deal. (Use the newspaper or go online to check.)

6

How to Lose All of Your Money Without Really Trying

In the nineties, tracking the stock market became America's greatest spectator sport. It wasn't too long ago that people chatted up companies the way they used to talk about baseball teams. Investing in stocks seemed like a one-way ticket to wealth. We all know the stories of people our own age suddenly becoming instant I.P.O. millionaires. Though we may not have even known what I.P.O. stood for, we knew what a millionaire was. We wanted to be one, too.

Well, what a difference a year and a few dozen accounting scandals make. Turns out that what the NYSE giveth, it also taketh away. During one four-month period in 2002, the Dow Jones Industrial Average declined almost 30 percent (see chart, page 100), obliterating trillions of dollars of investors' money. One thing we've learned from all of this turmoil is that no one can predict the future. No one, from Alan Greenspan to, umm, George W. Bush, could foresee such a dramatic reversal of fortune coming. However, it's probably safe to assume that the runaway bull market of the last decade won't come raging back anytime soon.

People who came of financial age in the nineties picked up

some supremely dangerous investing habits. In a market where sticking a ".com" after a name could add 50 points to a share, it's easy to start believing that you've got the Midas touch. We forgot that common sense, thorough research, and risk awareness are ultimately the best investment tools.

Forget everything you thought you knew about the market. We're going back to basic training. Here I provide a nuts-and-bolts look at investing in equities. It won't tell you how much or what to invest—that's just too much responsibility for a person to bear in these rocky times. This chapter isn't designed to show you how to make money. Rather, it will show you how to hold on to it. For new investors, that can be a much more valuable lesson.

My hope is to slam the brakes on those overeager neophytes itching to get started before they're ready. That's a recipe for financial catastrophe. There was a time not too long ago you could be relatively ignorant financially and still make piles of money in the stock market. No more. Now you need a lot more than a "hot tip" and a margin account to cash out. The stock market version of "tulip fever"* is over.

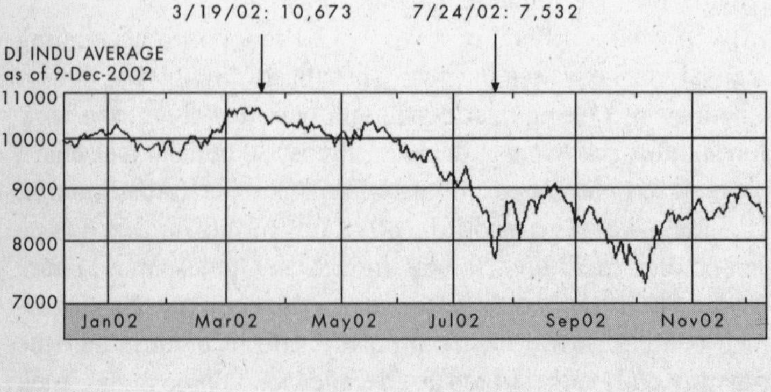

* A period in seventeenth-century Holland where speculation frenzy drove tulip prices to obscene levels.

STOCKS: THE BASICS

When you buy a share of stock in a company, you become a part owner in it. Companies issue millions of shares of their stock. These shares are in turn bought and sold by many different types of investors, from large financial institutions to the old lady down the street. Since a company can be worth billions and billions of dollars (called its market capitalization) the typical little guy's stake in any particular company borders on the infinitesimal. Still, being a shareholder, however small, gives you the same rights and profit opportunities as the mogul who owns millions of shares.

Before we talk about the different investment philosophies and the different ways to buy stock, you must understand the stock market tables. The tables are not unlike the Rosetta Stone of the financial pages. You can decipher a lot about a company from the stats the tables provide.

1. **52-Week High:** This number reflects the highest price the stock has traded in the past year. (Note how this differs from the year-to-date high, which marks the stock's high point from January 1 of the current calendar year.)

2. **52-Week Low:** Obvious, right? The lowest price of the stock over the last 52 weeks.

3. **Stock Name:** Usually an abbreviation of the company name. Though stock tables are listed alphabetically and use the full or partial company name, the actual ticker symbol can be quite different from the company name. Phillip Morris, for example, uses the symbol MO. Southwest Airlines trades under the symbol LUV. (Cute.) Most companies use a three-letter symbol, but not all. Coca-Cola equals KO. Explain that one.

   If you want to look up a company name but don't know the symbol, try the Internet. Most financial sites offer a

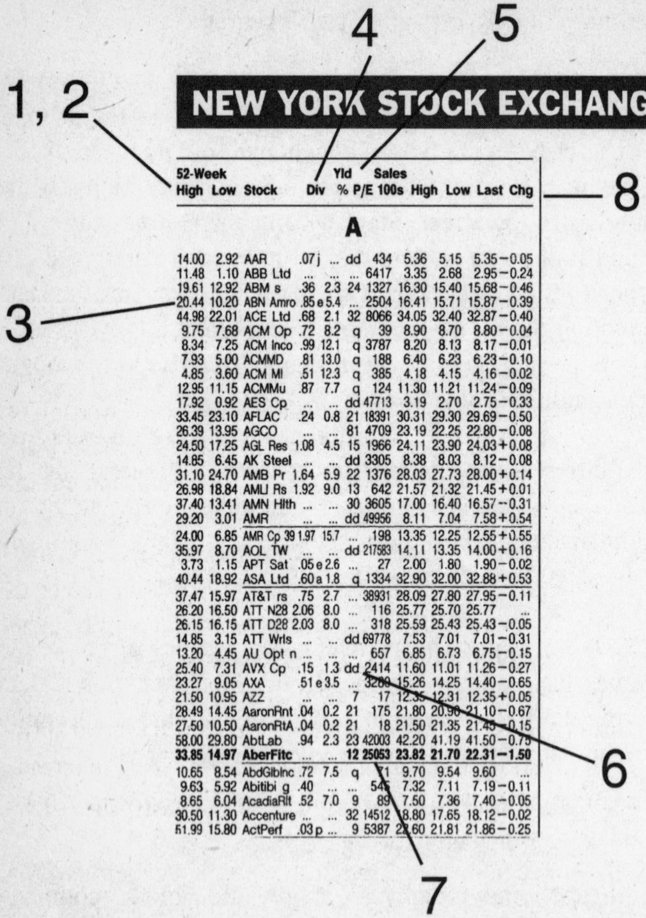

52-Week High	Low	Stock	Div	Yld %	P/E	Sales 100s	High	Low	Last	Chg
		A								
14.00	2.92	AAR	.07 j	...	dd	434	5.36	5.15	5.35	−0.05
11.48	1.10	ABB Ltd	...	...	...	6417	3.35	2.68	2.95	−0.24
19.61	12.92	ABM s	.36	2.3	24	1327	16.30	15.40	15.68	−0.46
20.44	10.20	ABN Amro	.85 e	5.4	...	2504	16.41	15.71	15.87	−0.39
44.98	22.01	ACE Ltd	.68	2.1	32	8066	34.05	32.40	32.87	−0.40
9.75	7.68	ACM Op	.72	8.2	q	39	8.90	8.70	8.80	−0.04
8.34	7.25	ACM Inco	.99	12.1	q	3787	8.20	8.13	8.17	−0.01
7.93	5.00	ACMMD	.81	13.0	q	188	6.40	6.23	6.23	−0.10
4.85	3.60	ACM MI	.51	12.3	q	385	4.18	4.15	4.16	−0.02
12.95	11.15	ACMMu	.87	7.7	q	124	11.30	11.21	11.24	−0.09
17.92	0.92	AES Cp	...	...	dd	47713	3.19	2.70	2.75	−0.33
33.45	23.10	AFLAC	.24	0.8	21	18391	30.31	29.30	29.69	−0.50
26.39	13.95	AGCO	...	...	81	4709	23.19	22.25	22.80	−0.08
24.50	17.25	AGL Res	1.08	4.5	15	1966	24.11	23.90	24.03	+0.08
14.85	6.45	AK Steel	...	...	dd	3305	8.38	8.03	8.12	−0.08
31.10	24.70	AMB Pr	1.64	5.9	22	1376	28.03	27.73	28.00	+0.14
26.98	18.84	AMLI Rs	1.92	9.0	13	642	21.57	21.32	21.45	+0.01
37.40	13.41	AMN Hlth	...	...	30	3605	17.00	16.40	16.57	−0.31
29.20	3.01	AMR	...	...	dd	49956	8.11	7.04	7.58	+0.54
24.00	6.85	AMR Cp 39	1.97	15.7	...	198	13.35	12.25	12.55	+0.55
35.97	8.70	AOL TW	...	...	dd	217583	14.11	13.35	14.00	+0.16
3.73	1.15	APT Sat	.05 e	2.6	...	27	2.00	1.80	1.90	−0.02
40.44	18.92	ASA Ltd	.60 a	1.8	q	1334	32.90	32.00	32.88	+0.53
37.47	15.97	AT&T rs	.75	2.7	...	38931	28.09	27.80	27.95	−0.11
26.20	16.50	ATT N28	2.06	8.0	...	116	25.77	25.70	25.77	...
26.15	16.15	ATT D28	2.03	8.0	...	318	25.59	25.43	25.43	−0.05
14.85	3.15	ATT Wrls	...	...	dd	69778	7.53	7.01	7.01	−0.31
13.20	4.45	AU Opt n	...	...	...	657	6.85	6.73	6.75	−0.15
25.40	7.31	AVX Cp	.15	1.3	dd	2414	11.60	11.01	11.26	−0.27
23.27	9.05	AXA	.51 e	3.5	...	3280	15.26	14.25	14.40	−0.65
21.50	10.95	AZZ	...	...	7	17	12.35	12.31	12.35	+0.05
28.49	14.45	AaronRnt	.04	0.2	21	175	21.80	20.90	21.10	−0.67
27.50	10.50	AaronRtA	.04	0.2	21	18	21.50	21.35	21.45	−0.15
58.00	29.80	AbtLab	.94	2.3	23	42003	42.20	41.19	41.50	−0.75
33.85	**14.97**	**AberFitc**	...	...	**12**	**25053**	**23.82**	**21.70**	**22.31**	**−1.50**
10.65	8.54	AbdGlbInc	.72	7.5	q	71	9.70	9.54	9.60	...
9.63	5.92	Abitibi g	.40	...	...	546	7.32	7.11	7.19	−0.11
8.65	6.04	AcadiaRlt	.52	7.0	9	89	7.50	7.36	7.40	−0.05
30.50	11.30	Accenture	...	...	32	14512	18.80	17.65	18.12	−0.02
51.99	15.80	ActPerf	.03 p	...	9	5387	22.60	21.81	21.86	−0.25

stock look-up function or symbol guide, which can spit out the symbol when you plug in the name of the company. It's always a good idea to make sure you've got the right symbol before you buy stock. There are many tales of people who meant to buy Microsoft and ended up owning something like MisterSoftee instead.

4. **Dividend:** This is the annual amount per share you receive from the company. Dividends are paid to shareholders

each quarter, and may be taken in cash or reinvested to buy more of the company's stock. Dividends vary dramatically, with many companies paying 5 or 6 percent of their share price in dividends and many others paying none at all.

Generally, companies that pay large dividends tend to be established, stable companies whose rapid-growth days are behind them. To keep their stock attractive to investors, companies turn their profits directly over to their shareholders instead of using the money to expand and for R&D. The share prices of these companies tend to be less volatile compared to the rest of the market. Newer, more rapidly growing companies rarely pay dividends, preferring to use the money to fuel growth. In theory, shareholders benefit from a higher stock price that is supposed to accompany additional growth. That's the theory, anyway.

Dividends are important, but they are but one factor in picking stocks smartly. Some stocks, for example, may pay a very high dividend in relation to the price of the share, but for disturbing reasons. The stock price could be depressed because the company is having financial difficulties. Besides the heightened risk of investing in a troubled company, you also might lose the dividend as the company slashes it to preserve cash.

But you can't assume that a stock with a generous dividend won't rise considerably in the future. To cite one example, a few years ago, tobacco litigation spooked investors away from Phillip Morris. The stock sunk to around $18 a share. The company, still healthy and profitable despite the lawsuits, maintained its $2.12 dividend. Even if the stock didn't go up another penny, lucky investors who bought at that price realized an immediate annual return of almost 12 percent on their investment. (Compare that to the less than 1 percent interest many traditional savings accounts pay.) As if that weren't a great enough return, lawsuit concerns eased, and Philip Morris skyrocketed, hitting a high of $60 a couple years later. Cigarette smoking may be harmful to your health, but it can be pretty damn robust for your portfolio!

5. **Yield:** The yield is a handy way to calculate how substantial (or paltry) a dividend is compared to the price of the stock. It is the ratio of the annual dividend to the stock's closing price, expressed as a percentage. In the sample table above, Abbott Labs (AbtLab) closed at $41.50 and pays a dividend of $.94. If you divide 41.50 into .94, you get 2.3 percent, or Abbott's yield. Obviously, a company that doesn't pay a dividend cannot have a yield. (In the table, see AOL Time Warner.) Yields change daily with the stock's closing price. As a stock's price goes up, its yield will decline. If the stock declines, its yield goes up. As a shareholder, you are only concerned with the yield at the time of purchase.

6. **P/E Ratio:** The p/e, or price-to-earnings, ratio is the price of the share divided by earnings per share over the last four quarters. It is probably the most important column in the table. Some investors swear by p/e ratios as the only way to pick stocks. Others weigh it alongside many other considerations. Whichever camp you eventually fall into, it is a number not to be taken lightly. The p/e ratio can be an invaluable tool in helping you decide if a stock is undervalued, overvalued, or priced just right. It's a big concept to grasp, so let's try an example using nice round numbers:

   Say WidgetCo. has one million shares of stock outstanding. WidgetCo reports earnings of $1 million dollars for the year. To calculate the earnings per share (or e.p.s), you divide the earnings ($1 million) into the number of shares (1 million) to come up with an e.p.s of $1 per share. (If WidgetCo had earnings of $2 million, the e.p.s would double to $2 per share.) If the stock is trading at $10 per share, with an e.p.s of $1, the p/e ratio is 10 ($10 share price divided by $1 e.p.s.). If the stock is trading at $20, the p/e ratio would be 20. ($20 divided by $1.) P/E ratios aren't listed in negative numbers, so a company that reports a loss receives a "dd" in the column (such as AVX Cp). As you know from high school, "D's" are rarely good news, and no company can survive on losses forever. (Although a money-losing company should not be automatically shunned. "Young," promising companies often lose money before quickly turning profitable.)

This may seem a bit confusing initially, but even beginning investors can use a stock's p/e ratio to determine if a stock belongs in their portfolio. Just because a stock's p/e ratio seems out-of-whack compared to others in its category doesn't mean it should be avoided. But it should be given additional scrutiny. (Note: different industries have different average p/e ranges, so you are interested in a company's p/e in relation to its "peers.") Poor earnings and a high stock price will lower a company's p/e ratio; solid earnings and a depressed stock price will raise it. Find out why before you buy.

7. **Sales (a.k.a. Volume):** The number of shares bought and sold that day. The number is listed in 100s. That means for Abercrombie & Fitch (AberFitc) 2,505,300 shares actually traded hands. A quick scan of the sales column gives you a sense of the magnitude of trading that goes on each day on the various stock exchanges.

   Most financial websites let you compare the day's volume with the average number of shares traded daily. If a stock's trading volume is heavier than usual, there is usually a reason for it. The company may have issued an unexpected earnings report (either good or bad), an analyst may have upgraded or downgraded the stock, or an institutional investor might have bought or sold a large block of shares.

8. **High/Low/Last/Change:** With the ring of a bell, the stock market exchanges open promptly at 9:30 A.M. and close six and a half hours later at 4:00 P.M. During those hours, stock prices are in constant motion. Stocks move up and down, and rarely stay still for very long. The chart of this movement resembles a roller-coaster ride, hitting several peaks and valleys over the course of a single day. These columns record what is called the "intraday" high and low. Subtracting the difference between the two gives you the stock's trading range for the session. Think of the High and Low columns as daily versions of the 52-Week High/Low.

Just because a stock hits a certain price during the day, doesn't mean that is the price you can sell it at the close of the session. The final trade of the day is recorded in the "Last" column. That's the trade that counts. It is measured against the final trade of the previous day. The difference between the two is the number in the "change" column. Stocks that close higher are noted with a "+" sign. Declines are noted with a "—". The intraday highs and lows are not used when calculating the change in the stock's price.

The More I Learn, the Less I Know

The market is a fantastic place to invest your money, but it doesn't suffer fools lightly. Jump in before you're completely ready, and, sure, you might get lucky once, twice, maybe even three times. Eventually, however, you'll almost always trip yourself up. Becoming a smart investor is a lot like learning a foreign language. You can cram all you want the night before the final, but only time and regular study will make you conversational. The market has its own language, with unique rhythms and cadences that you must master before you become fluent.

If you insist on playing the market before you're truly ready, please—start small. Don't risk anything you can't afford to lose. Take $3,000 and open an online trading account. Then, read everything you can get your hands on that will make you a wiser investor. First stop: *The Wall Street Journal*. With nearly twice as many subscribers as *The New York Times*, the *Journal* is Wall Street's bible. It's much less starchy than you might think, and even has a terrific "Personal Journal" section that covers everything from must-have gadgets to cut-rate Caribbean vacations. (Lefties be warned: the editorial pages are a right-winger's wet dream. Skip those pages if you can't handle it, but don't dismiss the rest of the paper.) *Forbes*, *Money*, and *Barron's* are three pretty good resources as well. You won't comprehend everything at first, of course, but stay with it. In time, all of that finance speak will be as easy to digest as an article about Ben and J.Lo in *People*.

The Web offers a treasure trove of educational information for the inexperienced investor. Personally, I like MSN's Money section. It's well organized, accurate, and doesn't assume you wear a power suit five days a week. Other ISP's like Yahoo! and AOL offer helpful financial tutorials as well. If you want to research individual stocks, consider subscribing to hoovers.com, a comprehensive equities research site. While much of the content is free and helpful, the truly good stuff is available only to subscribers (about $99.95 annually). Once your investing levels start getting more serious, consider subscribing. The subscription-only content might keep you from making costly investment blunders far beyond the 99 bucks you tried to save.

LIBRARY

Hopefully you're getting the message. The market is no place for children. I strongly believe that you shouldn't sink a dime of your money into buying individual stocks until you're ready. The titles below will help you decide when you are ready. Beginning investors should let *caveat emptor* guide them more than *carpe diem*. Despite the fancy credentials of the authors, you'll notice they often offer starkly contrasting advice. This shouldn't surprise you. There are as many different investing philosophies as there are stocks. Reading these books will expose you to different ways of thinking about money and familiarize you with the language of investing.

Greed Is Good: The Capitalist Pig Guide to Investing, Jonathan Hoenig (HarperBusiness). Highly entertaining Gen X finance guide for those more familiar with *The Facts of Life* than the facts of money. Hoenig is the host of the syndicated radio show *Capitalist Pig*, which, full disclosure, I've never listened to. If it's anything like his book, however, prepare to laugh while you learn. Fonzie and *Jetsons* references abound.

A Random Walk Down Wall Street, Burton Malkiel (Norton). First published in 1973 and updated through three decades, Malkiel's book is something of a classic among investors. Brokers hate it, and it's easy to see why. Malkiel argues that no one can regularly predict short-term market movements, so don't waste time (and money) trying. However, since we know that over the long-term, market indexes such as the Dow Jones Industrial Average move ever upwards, Malkiel believes that tying your investments to one of these indexes is the best way to ensure reliable returns with the least risk. No *Happy Days* mentions, but highly readable nonetheless.

Bulls Make Money, Bears Make Money, Pigs Get Slaughtered, Anthony Gallea (Prentice Hall). Plain English advice for new investors broken down into lessons rarely longer than a page. Especially helpful is Gallea's chapter on how psychology influences investment decisions. Gallea's prose is about as complex as a Nancy Drew novel, but don't let the straightforward writing style fool you—Gallea's experience as a money manager gives him terrific insights into the investor mind-set. Make this your bedtime reading and each morning you'll wake up a little wiser.

Investing Online for Dummies, Kathleen Sidell (Wiley). If there's a Dummies guide for everything from back pain to knitting, why not one for investors looking to bypass traditional brokerage firms? At 386 pages, this guide will tell you much more than the average online investor will ever need to know about point-and-click trading, but the book also features an excellent guide for finding online investment resources to help you research individual stocks.

One Up on Wall Street: How to Use What You Already Know to Make Money in the Market, Peter Lynch w/ John Rothchild (Fireside). Anyone who's lost his shirt speculating in technology companies that produce things you need a Ph.D from M.I.T. to understand will definitely appreciate Lynch's basic premise. Like the subtitle says, Lynch, a big cheese Wall Street fund manager, believes that investors should stick to the companies they understand that make products they use. For Lynch, the power of observation is the best tool an amateur investor has to identify winning companies.

Stick with What You Know . . .

Legendary investor Warren Buffett has a simple rule when deciding what to invest in: Buy only what you understand. During the go-go tech boom, Buffett missed out on some pretty spectacular gains because he didn't understand how most of these companies could ever make money. But guess what? He also didn't lose his shirt during the great tech meltdown, when it became apparent that few of these companies would *ever* actually make money.

If Buffett, a man who's made billions choosing the right companies to invest in, can admit that he doesn't know everything, than you can, too. Even the most informed investor faces a large number of unknowns. Why stack the odds even further against yourself by taking a flyer on a company you don't understand? No one wants to miss the next Microsoft, but when you throw your money blindly at a stock just because everyone else does, you could just as easily be following them off the cliff. Don't worry that you'll miss that once-in-a-lifetime opportunity by bypassing companies you don't fully grasp. There are thousands of publicly traded companies in this country. There will always be another opportunity right around the corner.

Besides, just because you don't have a fancy M.B.A. doesn't mean your own instincts aren't right. Very often we know more than we think we do. Unfortunately, we let our insecurities as "amateur" investors undermine our otherwise sound judgment. I'm just as guilty as the next person. I could have avoided one of my very first big investment blunders had I listened to the little voice inside my head. Instead, I ignored it at a loss of several thousand dollars.

Restoration Hardware, the home furnishings chain, had just opened their first store in the city where I live. Since I was in the midst of my own home renovation, I eagerly stopped by, but left empty-handed. "There's nothing to buy," I complained to friends. I had little use for faux-'50s gardening gloves and overpriced leather club chairs I could get down the street for half the price.

Weeks later *The New Yorker* ran a lengthy, fawning profile of the company extolling the founder's brilliance in tapping into boomer nostalgia. The writer convincingly predicted great things for the company. Even though the article left me scratching my head—the merchandise didn't exactly seem to be flying off the shelves the day I visited—I didn't want to miss getting in on the next Pottery Barn. I loaded up on the stock at 14 and, well, you can probably see where this is heading. Three months later, the company announced major losses, the stock was trading at less than half of what I paid for it, and I dumped it. (I took some comfort watching the stock continue to crater after I sold my shares—the only thing more painful than losing money is losing more money.)

But Remember: Nobody Else Knows Anything

Say you want to get into the investing game, but don't have the time or desire to design a sound investment strategy for yourself. Lucky for you, Wall Street is teeming with talented, prescient experts available to offer you fail-safe advice that will make you rich beyond your wildest dreams. Not. Below are actual quotes from five different stock analysts. If you had bought 100 shares in each based on their recommendations, take a look at how your portfolio would fare just one year later:

Stock	What They Said, August 2001	8/2001 Price	8/2002 Price	Loss
Calpine	"Calpine still looks amazingly cheap at current prices."	$39.25	$3.03	–$3,622.00
Novell	"We think Novell has little downside risk, with huge upside."	$5.00	$1.97	–$303.00
Tommy Hilfiger	"This could be a chance to buy Hilfiger on the cheap."	$13.18	$12.60	–$58.00
Capital One Financial	". . . [T]he company's strategy will keep it growing quickly in the future and enable Capital One to maintain its position as the dominant market-share taker in the country."	$60.00	$27.70	–$3,230.00
AMR Corp. (American Airlines)	"Next year is going to be a very good year for the sector."	$37.50	$9.44	–$2,806.00

These are pretty hefty losses for any young investor, and I didn't even mention such former analyst darlings as Enron, Worldcom, and Tyco. (Yes, American Airlines was hurt by 9/11, but the stock has been pummeled more by business travelers' growing resistance to plunking down $4,000 for a domestic ticket.) These five examples are typical of the hit-or-miss nature of analyst's roulette. New investors, insecure about their own investment skills, often find it tempting to put absolute faith in the words of the so-called experts. They turn on CNN or CNBC, see some paunchy middle-aged guy rattling off a few stock names, and assume that his words carry the weight of God.

The cold, hard truth is that when it comes to investing, it's like what somebody once said about Hollywood executives: "Nobody knows anything." Some analysts, of course, have better track records than others, but *no* analyst gets it right 100 percent of the time—not even close. How will you know whether he or she is on target this time? Professionals have good and bad years. Put too much faith in a single expert on an off year, and you will regret not sticking your money under the mattress instead. For every analyst who's screaming, " Buy X," you can turn around and find another shouting, "Buy Y." "Tech is undervalued." "Tech is overvalued." Oceania is at war with Eurasia. Oceania has always been at war with Eurasia.

Savvy investors know to take analysts' advice with a grain of salt. They know that few offer completely objective research. Many brokerage firms in the nineties turned out to be all too willing to compromise their stock research in pursuit of lucrative consulting and underwriting fees. There have even been cases of honest analysts getting fired after an angry CEO complained about a negative report on his company. Rare is the analyst who will put a flat-out "sell" recommendation on a stock. One recent year, only 3 percent of publicly traded companies had an outright "sell" recommendation on them. You can bet that many more than that lost money for their investors.

With major Congressional corporate reform legislation in the works, Wall Street will have no choice but to clean up its act . . . somewhat. Already, the SEC is defanging some of the important changes. Journalists and legal advocates have noted loopholes and wiggle room that will prevent this critical legislation from going as far as it should. Regardless of how legislation impacts the market in the future, it's wise to remain skeptical of analyst predictions. Analysts are not Pre-Cogs. They do get things wrong. Ultimately, you are responsible for your own financial decisions.

Two Other Really Bad Ideas: Margin Trading and Shorting

Margin Trading

Used to be, you had to have money to make money. No longer. Through margin trading, almost anyone who wants to get into the stock market can borrow the cash to get started. It's a bad idea and you shouldn't do it.

Here's how it works: When you open an account, either through a brokerage house such as Merrill Lynch or through an online company such as E*TRADE, you will be asked if you want to "margin-enable" your account. Margin trading allows you to borrow a percentage of the amount of your original investment (up to 50 percent), so you can invest more than you have. So if you have $10,000 to invest, you could buy up to $15,000 in stocks. Of course, you don't actually own the entire $15,000 investment. You only have $10,000. The $5,000 must be repaid. You are wagering that your stock will rise so you can cover the $5,000 and pocket the difference.

But what if it doesn't? That's when margin trading can turn real ugly, real quick. When your stock falls and you've bought on margin, you lose money on shares you own but borrowed money to buy. Losses pile up much quicker. In the example above, say you wanted to invest in SureThing at $10 a share. Instead of buying 1000 shares with the $10,000 you have, you buy 1,500 shares on margin. Two days later, SureThing announces "accounting irregularities" (*uh-oh*) and the stock drops $3 a share. Your shares are now worth only $10,500. But you still have to pay the full $5,000 back. Deduct that from the $10,500 and you've got only $5,500 left of your original investment. With only a 30 percent drop in SureThing's stock price, thanks to margin trading, you've lost almost half of your original investment.

With one big exception, Rick, a 34-year-old manager of an upscale restaurant, has few regrets. But the one he has is a doozy. During the height of the Internet mania, Rick got caught up in the high-stakes world of day trading. "I set up an online trading account, dumped all of my savings into it, and started buying and selling on margin," he explains. "Because I work mostly nights, it was easy to sit in front of my computer during the day when the markets were open. That turned out to be my undoing."

Although Rick had his share of up days, he quickly discovered that day trading can cut a Sherman's March through your savings. "I would make big gambles on tech stocks, and I kept losing. But because the money was borrowed, I kept taking bigger and bigger risks to make it back."

Today, thanks to margin trading, Rick is in the hole for over $50,000. He's slowly paying it off, but he expects to be in debt until he turns 40. "It's set me back ten years," he says. "I can't afford a house, I have nothing for retirement—all because I drank the get-rich-quick punch."

You also pay interest on the money you borrow. The rate will vary depending on current interest rates. In a market paying single-digit annualized returns, interest can vaporize a healthy chunk before you've even started.

When stocks roared in the nineties, buying on margin seemed like an easy way to make money using other people's cash. The raging bull market of the last decade hid many of the pitfalls of the practice. When the market soured in recent years, many margin traders got burned. If a stock bought on margin falls too low, the lender has the right to make a margin call. This means you must come up with the cash to cover the loan. If you can't, the broker can sell your shares at the depressed price to make good on the loan, creating some pretty steep losses for you. (If it's any consolation, even the rich aren't exempt from margin trading's rigid requirements. Just look at the Bass family,

Texas billionaires who in 2001 had to unload 135,000,000 shares of Disney stock to make good on a margin call.)

Margin trading violates one of the most sacred tenets of investing: Don't invest more than you're prepared to lose.

Short Selling

Identifying stock market winners isn't the only way people make money in the stock market. It sounds shady, but plenty of people clean up by targeting corporate basket cases. These people use an advanced trading technique called "shorting." The actual process is a breeze—anyone with a margin trading account can sell short—but this simplicity conceals some very deep, very real dangers that you, as a novice trader, don't need to attempt. For now, leave short selling to the grown-ups.

Here's a simplified explanation of how short selling works: You strongly believe that Acme Tool & Die is about to hit the skids, taking its share price with it. With short selling, you borrow the shares from your broker. The shares are then sold, and the money is credited to your account. At some point, you must make good on the loan (or "close the short") by buying back the shares and returning them to your broker. If your instincts were correct and the stock has fallen, you can buy the stock back at the lower price and pocket the difference. However, if the shares rise, you must buy the shares at the higher price, and you must make up the difference. You lose money if the stock goes up.

Shorting a stock that you believe will fall seems to carry the same amount of risk as buying a stock that you think will rise. This is why many inexperienced investors get seduced by short selling. In reality, shorting is riskier than traditional investing. Here are some reasons why:

- **When you fight history, you usually get your ass kicked.** Shorting bets against the overall direction of the market.

The chart below tracks the Dow from 1930–2002. Note the consistent upward moving direction. Despite many periods of dips and slowdowns, the market seems almost magnetically drawn north. Short sellers are like salmon swimming upstream against the current—to get where they're going, they have to swim a lot harder than everyone else.

- **The sky's the limit (for losing money, that is!).** When you buy a stock, you can't lose more than your initial invest-

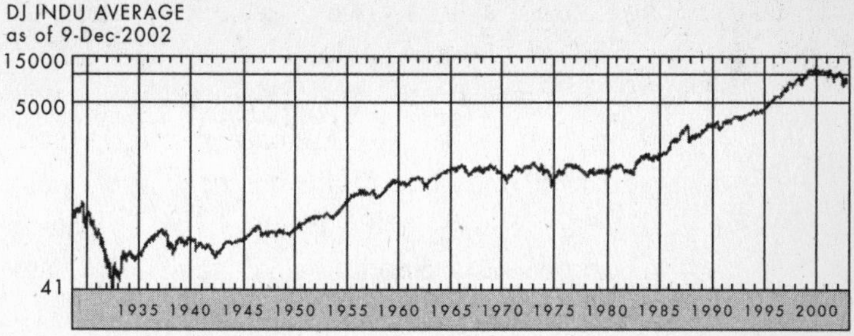

ment. If you buy a hundred shares of a company at $12 a share, and the company goes belly up, you're out your initial $1,200 investment. That's it. But say you short that same stock and the company experiences a dramatic turnaround. Stocks can't fall lower than $0, but theoretically they can climb forever. That $12 share could be trading at $80 before you know it. In the early '80s both Chrysler and Disney were on life support. Hard as it is to imagine, many analysts doubted either company would survive. But, to paraphrase Mark Twain, news of their demise was greatly exaggerated. Both companies had near-miraculous recoveries, with share prices for each increasing thirty and forty-fold over the years.

- **A call you don't want to be home for.** Because you are using borrowed money to short stocks, you risk getting the dreaded margin call should the stock rise. Just as in traditional margin trading, you must come up with cash quickly or liquidate. Some people who receive margin calls find themselves unable to come up with that kind of cash fast. Sudden liquidation, which denies an investor time to recoup his losses, becomes the only option.

- **The high price of genius.** Stock prices often trail reality. Your instincts about a company may be dead-on, but for reasons far too complicated to go into here, it sometimes takes a long time for a stock price to accurately reflect its true value. This is one time you don't want to be ahead of the curve. As you wait for the rest of the market to catch on to your brilliant foresight, you contend with interest payments, possible margin calls, even the (slight) possibility the broker might demand you cover the shares before you're prepared to. Short a bum company that happens to be in a hot sector during a bull market, and you may find yourself waiting *years* for the stock to sink.

You can think of short selling as Wall Street's answer to the office death pool. Each year you throw in your $20, positively, absolutely convinced that this is the year Ronald Reagan gets called to the great White House in the sky. But each year the Gipper defies the odds and rings in the New Year with Nancy. Meanwhile you've lost another 20 bucks waiting for the inevitable. At some point somebody will make money betting on Reagan, but, just as in the market, it's all in the timing.

For Those Who Just Can't Help Themselves: How to Trade Online

I realize that some of you are trigger-happy and won't wait until you're completely seasoned to start trading. This section is for you. In return, I ask for two things. Promise me you'll start small (no more than $3,000 to start with) and you will under no circumstances buy on margin. If you'll agree to those two things, read on:

True Do-It-Yourselfers bypass traditional brokerage firms altogether (along with their high commissions) and do it all from their laptop. Opening an online trading account is fast and easy, and for people confident enough in their investing skills, it offers most of the advantages of using a broker without the hefty commissions.

In the mid-nineties you couldn't turn on the television without seeing a barrage of ads hawking E*TRADE, Ameritrade, or a million other online firms. Many of those companies have since consolidated or folded, but you still have an array of options to choose from. We're talking about your money, here. How do you choose the best site?

I'll let you in on a little secret—it doesn't really matter. These are big businesses. You don't have to worry about some guy named Vinnie draining your funds and skipping off to South America. Most of the bugs have been worked out now so that system crashes are relatively rare. There just isn't that much difference in the services each offers. For example, Schwab offers clients stock ratings generated by computer and therefore free of analyst bias. Unfortunately, the jury's still out on whether the computer model is any better at picking individual stocks than its highly paid human counterpart.

You should be most concerned about two things when choosing an online broker: site navigability and cost per trade. Before you sign up with an online broker, do yourself a favor and take a tour of the site. For example, when you want to see how much you paid for a stock a year ago nothing is more frustrating than having to spend an hour trying to figure out how to access the information. As far as fees go, there should be a place on the site that clearly lists all fees and explains policies in plain English. If there isn't, think twice about using a brokerage service that's less than up front about something so basic. You should also check to see if there is a discount for electronic trade confirmation. All this means is that instead of getting a record of each transaction mailed to your house, the broker e-mails it to you instead. For some reason, many people feel more comfortable paying extra for written confirmation. This is silly. A printed e-mail will serve you just as well should you need a paper trail.

Once you've settled on a broker, you need to set up an account. This involves filling out an application that you can download and then depositing the minimum amount required. You can either pay by check or have the money deducted electronically from your bank account. Once the funds clear, congratulations—you're ready to start trading.

Online Broker Directory

Broker	Web Address	Phone Number	Commission*
Ameritrade	www.ameritrade.com	800 454-9272	$10.99
TD Waterhouse	www.tdwaterhouse.com	800 934-4448	$17.95
E*TRADE	www.etrade.com	800 387-2331	$14.99
Schwab	www.schwab.com	800 435-4000	$29.95
Harris*direct*	www.harrisdirect.com	800 825-5723	$20.00
Fidelity	www.fidelity.com	800 FIDELITY	$32.95

* Commission based on 15 market orders per year of 100 share blocks.

How to Do It

If you know how to click your mouse, you have the technical skills to buy or sell stocks online. This is how these sites make their money, so it's designed to be easy. However, there are some basic terms you need to know before clicking your way to Master of the Universe status:

- MARKET ORDER: With a *market order*, you buy the stock immediately at the best price available at that particular moment. Market orders are usually executed within seconds.
- LIMIT ORDER: Say you want to buy shares of Amalgamated Subterfuge. The stock currently trades at 40, but it is historically volatile. You think you can get it for less—around 37. What can you do? Place a *limit order*, which won't execute the trade until the price falls to 37 or better.

  Incidentally, you can place a limit order to sell a stock as well. With a limit sell order, you are commanding your broker to sell at a certain price, not buy. This type of order is useful if you believe a stock is trading near its high and is unlikely to climb much further.
- STOP-LOSS ORDER: No one has time to baby-sit his stock holdings 24 hours a day. If you do, maybe you need to get out of the house more. But if you're an active, already stretched-to-the-limit thirtysomething, you can't be spending every free minute fretting over whether you're the last to know that your company's CEO has just been thrown in the clink.

  A *stop-loss order* triggers an instant "sell" order should the share price of a stock fall below a price you determine in advance. Say you want to get in touch with your spiritual side by backpacking through Bhutan* for a month. You also don't want to come home broke. You're worried that your 200 shares of Hi-Wire Telecom might plummet while you're in the mountains learning to goatherd. What

* Bhutan: Tiny land-locked kingdom sandwiched between Nepal and Tibet. Population 1,232,000. Bhutan got its first television set in 1999—just in time for *Alias*!

can you do? You could program your online account to sell should the stock fall below a pre-set price. Say Amalgamated currently trades at 45. You decide you want out at 40. If the stock goes up, you'll come home still owning those 200 shares. But if it dips below 40, no worry . . . you'll still come home with a cool $8,000 waiting in your account.

When placing a stop-loss or a limit order, you'll also need to specify whether the order is a day order or GTC (good 'til canceled). A day order expires at the end of the trading day. A GTC order remains in effect until it is executed or you cancel it. (Note: some online brokers cancel GTC orders at the end of the month they were placed. The policy should be explained on the website.) GTC orders offer a reassuring peace of mind—you place the order and then forget about it (or backpack through Bhutan). Sometimes, however, a GTC can come back to bite you.

Say you own 300 shares of Casey Pharmaceuticals. The stock currently trades at 60. You place a GTC limit order to sell if Casey Pharmaceuticals goes up to 70. Six months later, the company announces it's discovered a cure for the common cold. The stock shoots up to 90. Before take your windfall and head over to the Land Rover showroom, check your balance. That forgotten GTC limit order you placed last January did what it's supposed to do and dumped everything at 70. Don't despair . . . I'm sure the Kia dealer down the street has something in the perfect color with your name on it.

Fearless Factor

- *Start slowly.* This is the best advice for new investors you'll ever read. The market eats unseasoned investors for breakfast. Take the time to familiarize yourself with the financial markets and you'll avoid the mistakes of those who have gone (broke) before you.

- *Analysts' recommendations are not the final word in equities investing.* But they very well may be half-baked, misleading, or downright dishonest. Follow up on any individual stock pick with your own thorough research.

- *Don't invest in companies or industries you don't understand.* Take a cue from Warren Buffett: there are enough pitfalls out there in the business world. Why complicate your odds by investing in stocks you can't properly assess? There are plenty of opportunity in stocks that you can.

- *Say no to margin trading and shorting.* They can be disastrous for beginning investors. Don't even think about it.

- *Online trading can be a viable option for individual investors.* Just be sure to familiarize yourself with the trading terminology before you begin, and resist the urge to buy and sell recklessly. (And don't "margin-enable" your account.)

7

Eight Surefire Rules for New Investors

Keep these front and center before you start investing and you'll avoid many of the common mistakes all beginners trip themselves up on. (Yes, including me. I said "all," didn't I?)

Rule 1: Fall in love with your partner, not your stocks. As strange as this sounds, many investors develop more than a fiscal attraction to the companies they own. They become emotionally attached to their investments. This not uncommon syndrome can plague investors at all levels. However, inexperienced investors, like awkward adolescents experiencing the first nips of puppy love, are especially vulnerable. First comes infatuation, when your stock can do no wrong. If it falls on bad news, you'll make an excuse and forgive it. Others may see your stock for what it is and wisely cut bait, but you hold on, refusing to admit betrayal. Love is blind—the market isn't. Don't get attached to your investments.

Rule 2: Stocks can* always *go lower. Technically, I suppose, that's not true. A stock can go to zero. If that happens, it's called bankruptcy, and there's no coming back. Hopefully, you've divested by then.

Many young investors choose stocks as if they were browsing the aisles at Target. In the quest for bargains, price becomes the paramount consideration. While the theory may be perfectly valid—find stocks that have hit bottom, and wait for them to go back up—they often use a dangerous and simplistic "methodology" to implement it. These naïve young things simply look at the 52-week high/low, see that the stock is trading near its low, and assume it will climb back up. So they load up on the "bargain," thinking at some point it must return to its high.

While it's true that stocks drift upward and downward—sometimes without rational explanation—most of the time there are very good reasons why a stock has been beaten down. People who scour the market looking for undervalued stocks are called value investors. A seasoned value investor looks at far more than the company's stock price in determining whether the stock is cheap or not. Among other things, he will compare the stock price to others in the sector, and consider whether there are any temporary, correctable factors holding down the share price. But choosing a stock based solely because its scraping bottom is a dangerous game. You may very well find the so-called bottom is just a temporary stop on the way to new depths.

Rule 3: But stocks can also go higher (and higher). There is no preset ceiling on a stock. Just because a stock is trading near its historical high doesn't mean all of the gains have been squeezed out of it. A long extended upward line on a stock chart may indeed give a prospective investor pause. We all know the laws of gravity—what goes up must come down, right?

Don't tell that to the people who bought Krispy Kreme in early 2000. As the chart below indicates, long-sighted investors rode a one-way ticket to big gains. With a few brief dips, the stock has been one big glazed joyride for investors. An original $1,000 investment in early 2000 sold nine months later would double your money. Not bad. A thousand bucks is a thousand bucks. But if you held on to those shares for just another two years, those shares would be worth a hot $18,000!

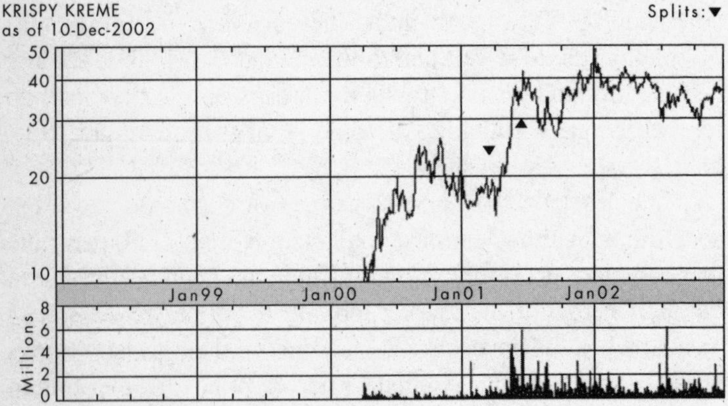

Splits: 3/20/01 (2:1); 6/15/01 (2:1)

Same with Starbucks. Had you invested $1,000 in Starbucks in the early nineties, you could have cashed out two years later for a cool $7,000 profit. But then you would have lost out on the additional *$240,000* those shares would be worth today if you held on to them.

Rule 4: If you want glamor, read a magazine. Admittedly, reading the annual report of some glitzy media conglomerate is a lot more exciting than reading the shareholder's report of, say, a waste removal company. But you don't buy stocks to have fun. You buy stocks to make money. Many an impressionable investor has been seduced by the sex appeal of so-called "glamor" stocks, only to learn the hard way that there is nothing glamorous about being poor.

This is not to say you should eschew entire sectors just be-

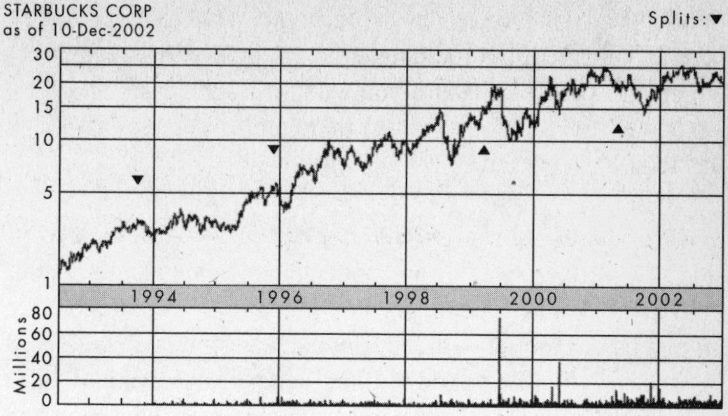

Splits: 9/30/93 (2:1); 3/22/99 (2:1); 4/30/01 (2:1)

cause they're *au courant*. Luxury goods, entertainment, and the Internet (*really!*), have often proved to be spectacular investments. You should, however, examine the reasons for your own attraction to the stock. In this treacherous market, stodgy, established, and consistent may turn out to be the sexiest combination out there.

Rule 5: Don't dis the dividend. Throughout the '90s, investors were trained to look at one thing and one thing only: the share price, and how quickly it was climbing. When a stock could double and triple within months, the once noble dividend became little more than chicken feed.

But that was then, this is now. We're living in a new decade of diminished expectations and lower gains. Dividends offer dependable, if not spectacular, returns. That's important in a volatile, punishing market, where you might end the year exactly where you started (if you're lucky.) Sure, a 3 or 4 percent yield isn't going to make you rich, but it might be the only thing keeping you ahead of inflation.

If a stock pays a decent dividend, consider reinvesting it. This option allows you to take payment in the form of additional stock. If you own 100 shares of a stock that pays a quarterly dividend of 50 cents, instead of receiving a check for $50, you take it in stock. Over the course of a year, you'll own another $200 in stock. Chances are you won't miss the cash, and it's a smart way to continue to invest in a company that you believe has long-term potential.

Rule 6: Pigs get slaughtered at the market. With the exception of your therapist, no one understands human nature better than a Las Vegas casino. Casinos make billions catering to a simple basic emotion—greed. Long ago casino owners figured out that people like only one thing better than cash, and that's more cash. It's why so few people are able to walk away when they're ahead of the game, and why so many hot streaks end in heartbreak. If you've ever gambled, you know that feeling. You're up a few rounds, doing well. You tell yourself you'll cash in your chips after a few more rounds—it seems a shame to stop now. What if you're leaving the game too early? You might win again. What harm is another round? Wouldn't another couple hundred dollars in winnings be nice? So you roll the dice, hope for the best, and, well . . . you're leaving Las Vegas a broken man.

You can avoid the perils of gluttony by choosing a "sell" price at the time you buy, and sticking to it. You don't want to fall prey to the "just a little more" trap, which can blind you from an otherwise reasonable assessment of a stock's continued upside. Adam learned this lesson the hard way: "I read an article about this company, saying the stock was unjustifiably cheap. I did some research and it checked out. I looked at the historic p/e ratios and the trading range for the last two years. It looked like a good investment. So I bought a ton of the stock at 18, and told myself I would sell it if it hit 30. It took some time, but it eventually did. But I didn't sell. I just pushed my original number up a bit. I told myself I'd sell when it hit 35! And it did! I had made over $5,100! So I told myself, 'I'm on a roll, I'll sell at 40.' But it never got there. It started dropping, but I couldn't let go. I wanted my $5,100 back! So I held and held, and now the stock is at $20. I'm still up $600, but when I think about how much more I could have made, I go crazy."

You can also get greedy in reverse as well. The same way a losing gambler will try to pull his way back to zero, a desperate investor will hold on to a stock the rest of the world has written off as a loser. Cutting your losses may hurt, but the market isn't really sensitive to your pain. In determining whether to hold on to a declining stock, the price you paid should not be a consideration. A stock will rise or fall regardless of whether you paid $30, $40, or $60 a share for it. The price you paid is immaterial to its future stock price.

Instead, look at the factors driving the stock down. Is there new competition that poses a long-term threat to the company? Has the management team triumphed over similar setbacks in the past? These are some of the questions you should be asking yourself. One financial consultant I know suggests asking yourself if you were investing today, would you buy the stock at its current price? Asking for divine intervention, while understandable, has proven to be generally ineffective.

Rule 7: Celebrate diversity. Take a lesson from Enron. A tragically large number of Enron employees, guilty of nothing more than believing in the integrity of their bosses at the top, sank every penny of their life savings into Enron stock. For a while, the strategy worked. Enron stock doubled and tripled. With the company promising nothing but clear blue horizons in the future, Enron employees saw little reason to change course. Enron boldly hailed itself as "the greatest company in the world."

Cut to Fall, 2001. The shit hits the corporate fan. Enron discloses major accounting irregularities, and the stock begins its rapid descent to pocket change. Countless Enron employees, many in their fifties and sixties, are left holding the bag. And there's nothing in it.

Think this is an extreme example? See how the shares of former high-flyers Global Crossings, Worldcom, and Adelphia Communications are doing, if they haven't been de-listed by the time this book is published. Just months before these companies crashed and burned, analysts and investors considered them home runs.

Regardless of how confident you are in a company's prospects, it will always be vulnerable to forces beyond its control. If the sector falls out of favor with investors, for example, your stock may be dragged down along with the competition. It doesn't seem fair, but, hey, that's life. (Remember how your parents would punish all of you when only your bratty brother did something wrong? It's kind of the same thing.)

Many novice investors think diversity only guarantees smaller returns. They view diversification almost as a kind of compromise. "Since stocks rise and fall at different times," their line of reasoning goes, "aren't I just ensuring losses mixed in with my gains?" But picking stocks isn't a zero-sum gain—for every stock in your portfolio that gains, another one doesn't automatically fall. Sure, it's rare for every stock in a diverse portfolio to rise in a single day. However, if you've bought solid companies in diverse sectors, over the long run your portfolio should experience nice, healthy gains with less volatility. One or two dogs in a well-managed, diverse portfolio won't kill you. One or two dogs with nothing else will.

Rule 8: Keep your eye* off *the ticker. Anyone who's obsessively checked her e-mail 100 times or called her answering machine every hour to see if *he*'s called knows it doesn't guarantee that he will. It just makes the day go by slower.

With most of us never more than a few clicks away from Internet access, it's tempting to compulsively check in on how our investments are doing. Resist. First of all, your boss won't like it if he catches you spending your entire day on Yahoo Finance. But more importantly, too much attention to the market can distort your sense of time. You become hypersensitive to every bump and pothole the market hits. As legions of day traders learned the hard way, the market punishes the trigger-happy.

Since 1925, stocks have provided an average annual return of almost 12 percent. Through good times and bad, war and peace, bull markets, bear markets and everything in between, the market over the long haul has rewarded patient investors with double digit returns. Compare that to the .5 percent the bank down my street offers for saving accounts. Thanks, but no thanks. With a 78-year track record on its side, I'll take my chances on the market.

Not every stock will be a long-term winner, of course. Many companies never even make it to the finish line. (Later you'll learn how you can protect yourself from plunging stock prices when your back is turned.) But for the serious, long-term investor (which, you, as a young thirtysomething with many more years on Planet Earth, *should* be) there is no more reliable, time-tested strategy than "buy and hold." Your goals would be better served knowing you've made solid long-term investments than booting up your computer at 2 A.M. to see that Viacom fell a quarter. (By the way, even the U.S. government is looking out for you. Gains on stocks held less than a year are taxed at a much higher rate than those held for a year or more.)

* * *

If these last two chapters have scared the bejesus out of you, good—I've done my job. I don't want to permanently frighten you away from the market. I just want you to wait until you're fully prepared and ready for combat. Jump in anytime before that and you're almost guaranteed to become a market casualty.

"Hold on," you say. "I have cash now and it's burning a hole in my pocket. I may not be ready yet to play market roulette by myself, but I want in on this capitalism stuff too. What can I do?" For you, there are mutual funds. Mutual funds are so important to any beginning investor's portfolio, I devote a whole chapter to them. Millions of ordinary investors swear by them, and with good reason. It's much easier to beat the market's average return by choosing a few good mutual funds than a few individual stocks. Turn the page to learn how.

Fearless Factor

The Rules for New Investors: A Pocket Guide

- **First rule:** Fall in love with your partner, not your stocks.
- **Second rule:** Stocks can *always* go lower . . .
- **Third rule:** . . . but they can keep going higher as well.
- **Fourth rule:** Don't buy stocks solely for their sex appeal. There's nothing sexy about losing money.
- **Fifth rule:** In a sluggish or volatile market, dividend-paying stocks offer reliable returns.
- **Sixth rule:** Don't let greed cloud your otherwise sound judgment.
- **Seventh rule:** You can avoid disaster by diversifying your portfolio. Don't overload on one stock or sector.
- **Eighth rule:** Obsessive-compulsive behavior is a disorder, not a portfolio management strategy. Neurotically checking stock price movements can distort your perspective and cause you to make unsound decisions. When playing the market, think long-term.

8

The Feeling Is Mutual

Admit it. The last two chapters have left you a little numb. You're skittish. Maybe a little frustrated. I've put your intelligence and financial acumen on the line. "Someone's gotta be makin' money in the stock market," you say. "I've got a triple-digit IQ and great instincts. Why not me?" With apologies to Melanie Griffith, a mind for business and a bod for sin just don't cut it in this dog-eat-dog market. Especially when there's a safer, more effective—hell, even more convenient way to participate in capitalism's greatest floor show.

Welcome to the wonderful world of mutual funds.

You've probably heard the term thrown around here and there. In the mid to late nineties, you couldn't turn on CNN or flip a magazine page (unless you were reading *InStyle*) without coming across Fidelity or Janus or some other company hawking their wares. That's because the market for mutual funds is *huge* and, until the recent downturn, growing. Today, mutual funds manage about $5 trillion of investors' money. Even spread over millions of individual accounts, that's a lot of Benjamins. As the place to park their cash for the long haul, mutual funds have earned their rightful place in investors' hearts.

It's All Fun and Games Until Someone Loses $10,000

Some new investors embrace mutual funds from their first disposable dollar. Others learn their investing limitations the hard way. Randall falls firmly into the latter category. A 33-year-old thriving small business owner, Randall prefers doing things his own way. "That's just who I am," he explains. "I can't work for anyone else, and I like being responsible for my own fate." After a few lean years, Randall's business started making money, Randall decided to go it alone in the stock market. "I opened an online trading account, boned up on the money magazines and CNBC, and plunged right in. I loved the excitement of picking stocks, talking over my picks with friends. It was like a game." Unfortunately, "plunge" might also be the word you'd pick to describe the direction of Randall's equity. "An unmitigated disaster. For every stock that went up, four fell. I pride myself on my business skills, but in this case they just didn't translate. I lost thousands of dollars. And this was during the bull market, when you had to work extra hard to lose money."

Randall lost faith in his ability to pick the winners, but not in the market itself. "I know the returns stocks can bring over the years. I guess I just didn't buy those," he sighs. His solution? Four different mutual funds that emphasize diversification. "The market is still a rough place to be right now," he says, "but all four funds are outperforming the market. When things rebound I'm confident my funds will still continue to beat the market."

Mutual funds, in their simplicity, represent sheer brilliance. You, along with many other faceless individuals, pool your money into a giant fund that invests in stocks, bonds, cash or some combination of the three. Many beginners assume that you have fewer investment options if you go the mutual fund route. Not true. There are over 13,000 mutual funds out there to choose from—more than the number of individual stocks!

The Mutual Fund Smorgasbord

Choices . . . so many choices. People have different investment goals and needs. Mutual fund companies know this, so they offer a full range of options for the individual investor. I couldn't possibly cover every possible mutual fund category in one chapter, so let's stick with some of the biggest choices you'll have to make and weigh the pros and cons of each.

Active vs. Index Funds

This is probably the most important decision you'll have to make in deciding where to put your stash. These fund types are like night and day, so it's critical you understand the difference between them.

When you buy into an actively managed mutual fund, you are buying into a fund overseen by a living, breathing money manager. This individual has wide berth in choosing the composition of the overall fund. She buys and sells individual stocks as she sees fit. Depending on the turnover in the fund, the composition of stocks at the beginning of the year may bear little resemblance to the portfolio at the end of the year.

Index funds, on the other hand, are managed passively, mostly by computer. Many investors find this vaguely unsettling. They imagine a lone computer in a dark room, sliding billions of dollars this way and that, not a human being in sight. This image, while creepily Orwellian, isn't quite accurate. Index funds have managers. They just do much less than their active counterparts. Dramatically less. With an index fund, your money is tied to the fate of a particular index, such as the S&P 500 or the Wilshire Total Market. A quick glance at the S&P 500 from 1980 to the present shows you why this is not a bad wagon to hitch your cash to:

PERFORMANCE OF S&P 500 INDEX 1980–2002

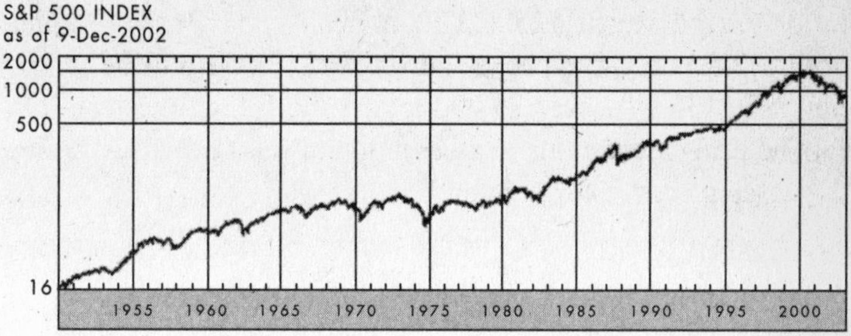

Actively managed funds can be extremely profitable—when run by a good fund manager. Separating the good managers from the bad, as I'll explain later, is no easy feat. Today's fund wizard is often tomorrow's dunce. Plus, statistics are not on the active fund's side. Hold on to any index (or passive) fund for ten or more years, and studies show you'll beat three-quarters of all actively managed funds!

Active funds can make sense if you're investing during a down market and your investing goals are more short-term. As every shareholder who's owned stocks in the last few years knows, the market can be a cruel mistress. Index funds, by definition, take a beating alongside the rest of the market. But if you are invested in an actively managed fund, in theory you have a chance of outrunning the market. *In theory.* You also stand a good chance of losing more than the overall market.

Investing in active funds will almost always cost you more for the privilege. Your expenses are higher in two ways. First, it costs more to run an active fund. Those higher costs are passed on to you. Index fund expense ratios average about .2 percent. The annual fee for active funds can climb higher than 2.5 percent.

The difference between those percentages may seem inconsequential to you, but over the years it will take a big bite out of your returns. Remember, that fee is taken out of your *total* investment, not just your gains.

Consider this: assuming an annualized 10 percent return, $10,000 invested in a mutual fund with a .2 percent expense ratio will be worth $25,423.32 in ten years. But in a fund with a 2.5 percent expense ratio, that $10,000 will be worth only $20,135.99—over $5,000 less! (The S.E.C.'s website offers helpful calculations to assess mutual fund expenses. Go to www.sec.gov/investortools.)

"I have a history of staying in relationships even when it's obvious to everyone else that it's over, so it's no surprise that I hold onto stocks long after everyone else has dumped them," laughs Serena, a 36-year-old social worker. Serena, like the independent-minded Randall earlier in the chapter, initially preferred to pick her own individual stocks. Unlike Randall, however, her stocks usually proved to be winners, at least briefly. A stock would rise, but when her sharp instincts told her to get out, she found herself unable to hit the "sell" button. "I would do all this research before committing to a company, but once I bought into it, I could never sell, no matter how bad all the signs were."

Serena fell victim to rule number one in the last chapter: she developed an emotional attachment to the companies she invested in. Instead of selling when times were good, Serena would hold on out of a misplaced sense of loyalty, resulting in some very painful rides to the bottom. For Serena, the solution was to close her online trading account and invest in mutual funds. "When you try to explain it, it sounds weird," she admits. "But it's harder to 'bond' with a mutual fund. I don't know every company my funds hold, so it's easier for me to cut bait if they underperform. It's about numbers, and nothing else."

The other way actively managed funds cost you more is even less transparent than those pesky operating fees. Because they trade more frequently, actively managed funds generate higher tax bills. Index funds trade less frequently, so their portfolios tend to generate fewer taxable sales. The IRS applies the same laws to these institutional trades as it does to individuals. Stocks held less than a year get taxed at a higher rate than those held longer. In an up market, all that buying and selling means more money for Uncle Sam, and less for you.

Growth vs. Value

Animal lovers divide people into two camps. You're either a dog person or a cat person, and never the twain shall meet. Similarly, mutual fund companies divide investors into two equally distinct groups, growth investors vs. value investors. Whichever side of the fence you fall on will play a big part in determining the mutual funds that appeal to you, so it is vital to understand each side's philosophy.

Growth Investing: Growth investors invest in the potential of a company. They choose companies that they believe have a glorious future, and often pay a premium for the stock. A company may be deeply in the red, but have a market value in the billions. How does this happen? Wall Street is betting that in time the company's earnings will "catch up" and surpass the current stock price. The company may have an exciting new business model (Southwest Airlines), a patented technology (Intel), or simply a delicious product that's sweeping the nation (Krispy Kreme—I admit it; I'm obsessed). Southwest has a market valuation greater than all of the other major airlines *combined*. This seems hard to fathom at first glance. After all, the other airlines have more planes, fly millions more passengers a year, and have venerable brands dating back to the early part of this century. Southwest has ugly planes and until recently flew exclusively to unglamorous places like Tulsa and Lubbock. But, over the past few years the major airlines have lost billions, while Southwest posts sharply higher earnings each year and continues to gobble up market share. Southwest shareholders believe that the airline's march forward is inevitable, and are willing to pay more to go along for the ride.

Because growth investing requires a leap of faith, however measured, it carries some risks. First, you're not likely to find a growth stock that pays dividends. There's only one way to make money—stock price appreciation. Second, these stocks are historically volatile. That was less true in the nineties, when sticking a ".com" on your company name and promising to "build community" could quickly double and triple your share price. (Can you tell I once worked at an Internet company?) Investors in these stocks may not expect profits for many years, but at the first sign of slowing growth, watch out! That stock can tumble faster than Mariah Carey's career. And once the sheen is off a growth stock, it's very difficult for it to regain momentum. Did you see *Glitter*?

With technology stocks leading the charge, growth funds delivered spectacular results through the nineties. Alas, much of this growth turned out to be pure Internet–bubble fantasy—the result of pie-in-the-sky valuations and accounting chicanery. In today's climate, the numbers in a company's annual report might as well be written in invisible ink. Growth stocks carry heightened risk. Once the sleaze works its way through the system and tough reform laws go into effect, things will no doubt change. Until it does, however, no one can say with absolute certainty where the next corporate stock scandal is lurking.

If you want to get into these funds, but are a little bit scared of the risks involved, choose a growth fund that makes safer bets within the category. You can still reap the advantages of growth stocks, but the companies within these funds tend to be a bit more established than the traditional growth funds. Any mutual fund company will offer promotional literature explaining the different types of growth funds available.

Value Investing: On the opposite end of the equity investing spectrum sit the value investors. These people prowl the market hunting for bargains—stocks temporarily beaten down for one reason or another, or simply overlooked by the investing public. What creates a value stock? Lots of things. For example, to distract voters from a faltering domestic economy, say a U.S. president declares war on an already crippled Middle Eastern country. Hard to imagine, I know, but stay with me. Tourism always suffers during a war, and with it the tourism industry. Disney, with theme parks around the globe, gets hit particularly hard any time there's an international crisis. Once peace is restored, however, historically the share price bounces right back up to previous levels. A value investor might scoop up depressed Disney stock during a war, believing the dip in share price will eventually rebound to normal valuations.

For the individual investor, identifying true value stocks poses something of a challenge. A depressed stock price could indicate value, but it could just mean the company, well . . . sucks. Neophyte investors often have trouble telling the difference without the proper research tools and access to company executives. That's where a good fund manager comes in. He should have the experience and resources to separate the wheat from the chaff.

Global Swarming

Another practical advantage mutual funds offer over individual stock picking is the opportunity to get in on hot overseas action. The U.S. of A. isn't the only place that turns money into more money. In fact, over the past few years, many foreign markets have consistently beaten the American exchanges. Global and international funds enable you to invest beyond borders, and you don't even have to speak the language. Without these funds, you'd have to do a tremendous amount of work and research to invest overseas.

Say you get a tip from your Icelandic online pen pal. He manages a herring cannery, and confides that his company's herring exports are about to go through the roof. You want a piece of the exploding Icelandic herring industry. Your friend assures you it's a sure thing. "Insider trading be dammed," you tell yourself. "I'll triple my money by year's end." So what do you do? You can't relocate to Reykjavik, and good luck finding the Icelandic equivalent of E*TRADE.

If you're part of a global fund with Icelandic investments, there's a good chance your fund manager is well aware of herring's upside and has invested accordingly. You don't have to do anything but keep investing in the fund. Language fluency, time differences, currency fluctuations, intricate knowledge of foreign economies—who has time for this stuff? I certainly don't, and I doubt you do either. That shouldn't mean you have to miss out on great foreign returns. Get in on a country that's getting its economic act together, and the payoff can be huge.

A word of caution: In the same way that backpacking through the Khyber Pass is considerably more dangerous than hiking in New England, international investing can be a dicey proposition. Living in the most stable country on earth, we tend to forget the palace coups and boneheaded economic policies that can roil foreign markets. Most experts suggest you limit your overseas exposure to no more than 25–30 percent of your total portfolio.

Be wary of international funds that invest in just one country. Unless you've got enough money to withstand potentially big losses, you should avoid these funds. They're simply too risky. Because so many things can go wrong overseas, diversity is even more critical when it comes to foreign investing. Even if you read an article in the *Wall Street Journal* or some other financial rag trumpeting some country as the Next Big Thing, take a pass. Besides the fact that these predictions often turn out to be flat-out wrong (Argentina, anyone?), there is still no guarantee that your fund manager will choose that country's superstars. Better to spread the risk around.

Caps: Size Does Matter

Many mutual funds restrict their portfolios exclusively to companies that fall within a certain size parameters. Size in this case refers solely to the company's market capitalization, not the number of employees or revenues or number of Post-It notes in the supply closet. Companies are usually divided into one of three categories; small caps (less than $2 billion, *Playboy, Martha Stewart Omnimedia*), mid caps (between $2 billion and $10 billion, *Harrah's, Staples*) and large caps ($10 billion and up, *Gillette, DuPont*). At first, this may seem like somewhat arbitrary investment criteria—after all, large companies fail just like smaller ones do (and make a lot more noise when they do). A small bio-tech company in a suburban office park would seem to share little in common with an upstart coffee franchiser. There is, however, method to this particular madness.

Historically, small stocks outperform their big brothers. You won't realize as much in dividends, but as a whole small caps have a better appreciation track record. On the downside, $5 is a lot closer to $0 than $60 is. Smaller companies fail. Their fortunes can change with the wind. You can expect more volatile share prices than you get with the large caps. You may not want to stomach the daily ups-and-downs. If that's the case, supersize your mutual fund and go large cap. (By the way, there's nothing wrong with buying both large cap and smaller cap funds. Diversify. Diversify. Diversify.)

Money Market Funds

If mutual funds were people, these funds would be the equivalent of the girl next door. Other types of mutual funds might be sexier and tantalize you with the thrill of a wild ride. A money market fund won't take you to new highs, but it also won't take the money and run. Like the girl next door, stability and no surprises are its primary appeal. Sometimes, depending on your situation, that may be just what you need.

No thirtysomething should view a money market as a long-term investment vehicle. The return is simply too low to be a part of any realistic retirement plan. However, if your goals are more short-term, (if you're saving for a house or to open a business, for example) you don't want to tie your money up in a long-term investment or a volatile one that you may be forced to sell at a loss. I have been in just that position, and it's no fun, believe me. You must either take your losses on the investment or miss out on the thing you were saving for anyway. With a money market, you will never have to make that unpleasant choice.

So what are money market funds, anyway? Unlike traditional mutual funds, which play the bond and stock markets, money market funds typically make very safe short-term investments in solid entities such as government bonds. Money market funds lend money (yours) to only the most creditworthy institutions, and return the interest paid back to them in the form of dividends. The yield, which varies considerably over time, is usually about one to two percentage points higher than a traditional savings account, although the spread will depend on the current rate environment. Tax-free money markets invest in municipal bonds, but you should consider these equally safe.

Don't be put off if all this sounds a bit complicated. The dividend is expressed in percentage terms, so it's easy to compare the interest rate of your local banks to the return on a money market mutual fund. Furthermore, the price of each share is fixed at $1, so there's no messy converting to do. If you have

2,000 shares of a money market mutual fund, you have $2,000. Simple as that.

Some people worry that these funds are not FDIC insured like bank CD's, so instead they settle for the lower rates offered by a savings account. If you're still paranoid that Washington or General Motors might flake on their loan obligations, bear this in mind: In the last two decades only one money market fund lost money, and it was only about 5 percent—hardly enough to conjure up images of dust bowls and bank runs. While in theory anything can happen—hey, if John Ritter can have a hit television show in 2003, you can't rule anything out—it's probably a safe bet that your money will be just fine.

Money doesn't grow on trees. It also doesn't grow in checking accounts! Compare the following sample rates on an account with a $2,000 balance:

Bank	**Checking***	**Savings**	**Money Market**
Citibank	0%	.50%	.75%
Fleet	0%	.60%	.75%
J. P. Morgan Chase	0%	.55%	.55%
Wells Fargo	0%	.50%	.81%
Fidelity	N/A	N/A	1.14%
Schwab	N/A	N/A	.85%
T. Rowe Price	N/A	N/A	.81%

* Standard checking account with no minimum balance requirements.

Besides the higher yield, money market funds come with two other nice benefits. Many will grant you check-writing privileges. While this can be a useful financial management tool, I don't advise closing your old checking account just yet.

Typically, you can only cash checks for larger amounts—the standard minimum varies between $100 and $250. Most of us write checks for far less than that. (There is no minimum check amount at brokerage firms.)

After spending her twenties swimming in debt, Erica finally reformed her wicked ways and learned to live within her means. A few years later, the Los Angeles–based talent manager's career took off. Soon the 36-year-old former credit risk found herself flush with cash. Ordinarily surefooted, Erica didn't know what to do with her newfound booty, so she let the money stagnate in a low-interest savings account. "I had never had any savings, and I loved the security it brought me. It was such a novel feeling for me, and I was terrified of going back to the old days. I'm just not psychologically ready to trust the markets. I'm also considering buying a house soon, and I want to know that money will be there for me when I decide."

Erica's boyfriend Jeff suggested she move her money into a money market fund and enjoy the slightly better interest rates they pay. After he convinced her that a money market fund was almost as safe as her savings account, she relented. "He knows me well enough not to push me into something risky," she says. Besides, she adds only half-jokingly, "I'm so financially conservative now. If I lose money, I cannot be held responsible for my actions." Erica is earning more money on her savings, and she—and Jeff—can still sleep at night.

Second, depending on a wide range of factors such as your income and where you live, tax-exempt money funds may be a viable option for you. An adviser can help you determine if you're eligible or if it makes sense for you. (Tax-exempt funds pay a lower yield than taxable funds, but taxes are not owed on the interest.) Traditional financial institutions such as banks, brokerage firms, and mutual fund companies offer money markets. Mutual fund companies usually offer the best funds with the lowest fees, so start with them. Call their 800 number or go online to check their rates.

Sector Funds

Conservative financial planners avoid these types of funds, and with good reason. Rather than invest in a wide range of companies, sector funds invest in one industry exclusively, such as telecommunications or pharmaceuticals. This strategy defeats the whole purpose of a mutual fund, which is to diversify. While a sector fund will likely still hold stock in more companies than you could invest in as an individual, if an entire sector sinks on external factors, such as increased government regulation or litigation, you're out of luck. Sectors also fall out of favor with both institutional and individual investors for seemingly capricious reasons. Get stuck chasing the "hot dot" when Wall Street has moved on to the next trendy thing, and it'll be a lot more painful than admitting you still own that stupid Razor scooter you bought to look cool.

How They Make Money

It's a mantra we all grew up hearing around the Thanksgiving table: "You get what you pay for." If your parents were talking about buying a Volvo instead of a Yugo, they were on to something. If, however, they were talking about how they chose their mutual funds, well . . . I wouldn't be counting on a Ewing-sized inheritance.

We're trained to automatically view as suspect anything we can get cut-rate. "If it sounds too good to be true, it probably is," and all that. I know people who take great comfort in paying retail. They see that $300 shirt by the designer with the unpronounceable name, and think, "If it's hanging in Barneys, it must be worth it." These are the people mutual fund marketers *live* for (assuming they have any cash left over after that little cashmere Jil Sander number).

You invest in a mutual fund to make money. Therefore, a top priority in choosing a fund should be minimizing the fees you pay to invest in one. Or, viewed another way, every dollar you pay in expenses is one less dollar of profit. If you're not savvy about the funds you choose, you could end up paying fees each time you buy, sell, or hold a fund.

Load funds are funds that pay a commission to the brokers and salespeople who convinced you that their fund is superior than all those other low-rent, no-load funds. With commissions as high as 5 percent, they'll have to be more than just a little better. Think about it. Say you sign up for a fund with a load of 5 percent and invest $10,000. If the fund breaks even, you're out $500. If it returns 10 percent, after the sales load, you've made a whopping $500 the first year. *Yippeee . . .*

Now, if load funds historically provided better returns than their no-load counterparts, than you could justify paying that commission for the promise of greener pastures. But here's the rub: they don't. There is absolutely no correlation between load funds and higher returns. Brokers often argue that load funds have more money to hire more talented fund managers. Frankly, that's a load of crap. After you factor in commissions and higher operating expenses associated with load funds, most load funds actually trail the no-loads. Also beware of back-end loan funds, which tack the commission on when you sell the mutual fund. Many back-end loan funds will waive the commission provided you hold onto the fund for a designated number of years (usually five). While this may seem fair, be careful. You shouldn't be penalized for rescuing your cash from a losing mutual fund by selling early.

Operating expenses, expressed as a percentage of your investment, are the other major expense associated with investing in mutual funds. You pay ongoing fees for as long as you own the shares in the fund. Someone's gotta pay for Mr. Big Shot Manager's massive salary, his limo, the research department overhead, the printing and mailing of all those prospectuses, etc. That someone is you. It's easy to forget about these fees because they're deducted before you're paid any return, but they're there. Also be on the lookout for a high 12b-1 fee (a.k.a. management fees), which is just an odd name for the fee that covers advertising and marketing costs.

Operating expenses are unavoidable, but you have tremendous leeway in keeping them as low as possible. Mutual fund companies must disclose their operating expenses in the fund's prospectus. Don't treat the prospectus the way you did your cell phone instruction manual and toss it into a drawer, ignored, unloved and unread. This being Wall Street, there's plenty of room for monkey business. Have you ever checked out of a hotel only to get hit with all those infuriating extra fees, such as the "city tourism development tax" and calling card surcharges? You might experience the same sticker shock if you don't fully understand the expense structure of your fund.

Sometimes companies will temporarily waive or lower their operating expenses (the equivalent of running a sale) on certain funds. You may get a few months at a discount, but turn your back and that percentage shoots right back up to its usual snow-capped heights. Always read the fine print, and if in doubt, call the company and speak to a representative.

How You Make Money *(You Hope!)*

You make money in mutual funds the same ways you make money investing in individual stocks. It's "buy low/sell high" on a grand scale, possibly with some nice dividend action thrown in to boot.

It's always good when a stock goes up, but when it's a stock you hold in a mutual fund, there are two possible ways to realize the gain. If the portfolio manager sells the stock for more than he paid for it, you receive the profit through *capital gains distributions* paid annually. You either receive a nice check from the fund, or you can elect to invest the profit back into the fund. (Of course, if the manager has sold more stocks at a loss, you get nothing. Worse, a fund can have capital gains from a stock the fund has owned long before you came onboard. You can lose money that way as well.)

Some of the stocks in the fund will likely pay dividends. Those dividends belong to you and all of the other shareholders in the fund. Again, you can take the dividends as a payment, or you can reinvest them. Generally speaking, most thirtysomethings should automatically reinvest their profits from dividends and capital gains. You're *investing*, right? Those gains should go toward building an anxiety-free future, not a fabulous diving vacation in the Caymans.

Hopefully, most of the stocks in your mutual fund will appreciate over time. If they do, the share price of the fund will rise alongside them. You don't realize these gains until you sell the fund. You can track the share price in the business section of any good newspaper. The mutual funds listings look very similar to the regular stock tables, and usually appear on the pages after them.

In choosing a mutual fund, the most important factor for you to consider is the way it generates returns—dividends, appreciation, or capital gains. If you are a conservative investor, you might prefer a mutual fund made up of stable, established companies that pay generous dividends. Over time, the share price of the mutual fund is less likely to increase substantially, but the steady dividends will provide reliable returns. Likewise, you might prefer a fund that actively trades stocks, in the hope that the manager can ride the momentum of the market. You may very well experience more dramatic returns, but be prepared for a higher tax bill come April 15.

If you're an indecisive middle-of-the-roader who wants it both ways, consider a fund that offers both growth and income. These funds hold some growth stocks, but they also invest in companies that pay dividends. They may also invest in bonds, which will pay you interest. With these funds, essentially you get it both ways. You lose out on the potentially fat returns of a pure growth fund, but you also have less reason to worry your portfolio will crash and burn. Plus, you have the additional safeguard of dividends and interest, which you should automatically reinvest if you are looking to grow your principal and not income.

What to Look for in Choosing a Fund

The mutual fund forest is a vast and potentially overwhelming one. There are literally hundreds of mutual fund companies in the U.S., offering funds of every shape and size. How can you possibly choose the best one for you? At least with individual stocks, you can familiarize yourself with the company, bone up on the company's reports, compare its current p/e ratio to its historical one, etc. Mutual funds, with their vast holdings, don't really enable such direct, do-it-yourself research. Naïve people, who nevertheless know the value of investing in mutual funds, fall into the biggest trap known to fund-kind. They read a profile of some manager "superstar" whose fund returned 35 percent last year, pile their life savings into his fund, and smack their lips at the anticipated bounty. Then the fund drops 20 percent in six months, and Mr. Stunned Investor concludes God hates him.

The truth is, God has other things on his mind than thinking about ways to wreck your mutual fund. If Mr. Stunned Investor had only done some research, he would know that when it comes to mutual funds, past is definitely not prologue. Study after study shows that top-performing mutual funds rarely keep it up over the long haul. Buying into a fund that had a stellar year might turn out to be the equivalent of buying a stock at the top of the market. Sure, it could still rise, but it might also be headed for a painful correction.

So steer clear of the superstars of the mutual fund world. Too often they turn out to be more like shooting stars, briefly burning up the sky before crashing down to earth. Instead, you should be looking for a fund that is in line with your investment strategy and run by an experienced manager with a consistently satisfactory track record. Many advisers suggest you stick to the larger fund companies, reasoning that they have better research tools at their disposal. This may or may not be true, but there's another reason to go with a large company that any harried thirtysomething will appreciate: convenience. We all have our own tolerance for paperwork. I don't know about yours, but mine is pretty damn low. Sticking with one fund family means that your reports will be listed on one statement, a big plus for those constitutionally opposed to diligent record-keeping. You can do everything you need to do by calling one 800 number instead of four. Transferring money between funds is a breeze if the accounts are in the same family. Also, if you buy a load fund and stay in the same family, you are eligible for "breakpoints," or discounted fees. As a new investor, you already have a steep learning curve. Make time to educate yourself by keeping the clutter to a minimum.

One final suggestion: if you're willing to lay out a little cash (about $11.95 a month) consider subscribing to Morningstar.com. This is mutual fund ambrosia. Here, you'll find everything you need to know about many mutual funds and the managers who run them. The site is devoted exclusively to mutual fund enlightenment, so you'll get your money's worth. If you want to become a smarter investor, but you're waffling on parting with the cash, remember—as an investment aid, the subscription fee is fully tax-deductible.

> Even when Jared started making good money in his late twenties, he still found himself with nothing left over at the end of each week. "It's amazing how there's always something to piss your money away on," says the 34-year-old graphic designer. "Here I was making three times the money I was making in my mid-twenties, and the only thing different was I could now pay off my credit cards each month." Fortunately, Jared realized that carrying a zero balance on his Visa isn't much of an investment strategy, so he wisely got the money out of his hands before he could squander it. "I set up a Fidelity account that deducts $300 from my checking account every week. I downloaded the paperwork online. It's the easiest thing in the world to set up, and now I know that no matter how dumb I am with the rest of my money, I'll have invested over $15,000 each year. It's very comforting."

Never Can Say Good-Bye

When it comes time to unload a mutual fund, knowing when to cut bait can paralyze even the most level-headed of shareholders. Nobody likes to sell any investment at a loss, but selling even a dog of a fund can be painful for many investors. Perhaps one reason is that mutual fund shareholders generally invest in funds for the long haul, so they question (and rightly so) whether they are pulling out prematurely. After all, no fund has an indefinite running streak. A dip, however small or temporary, hits even the best funds.

That said, there are a few signs that you can use to determine if it's time to cut your losses. If a fund underperforms its peers for several consecutive years, it may be time to throw in the towel and reallocate your investment. While a rebound is always possible, it is more likely you will earn better returns in a fund that has consistently delivered better results.

If you've invested in an actively managed fund that has delivered great returns in the past and the manager leaves, you may want to follow. If he's moving on to another company, consider shifting your money to his new employer (although you may incur additional taxes for doing so). After all, the fund manager is ultimately far more important than the letterhead on the firm's stationary. If, however, his successor shares his investing philosophy and experience, consider staying put.

Watch out for creeping expense ratios. The fees associated with managing mutual funds can be adjusted at any time. More often than not, fees are revised upwards, not in the other direction. (What a surprise!) If the fund is performing spectacularly, you should probably just eat the higher expenses. However, if it's not, it may be time to look elsewhere for a fund with a more reasonable fee structure.

Keeping a balanced portfolio may require you to reduce your holdings in a particular fund. I'll say it again—diversification is key. If you own several different funds, over time your holdings may become lopsided. This may be the result of a dramatic change in the valuation of the funds or changes in the make-up of the individual portfolios. For example, you notice that each of your funds is loading up on one particularly volatile sector, such as telecom. You may be willing to assume the heightened risk with one fund, but not all. In this example, you could lower your exposure by selling one of the funds and investing in a fund that doesn't own telecom.

Finally, the fund you originally bought may not be the fund you own now. How's that? Mutual funds are like apes. They evolve, often changing into something barely resembling the original. This change, called style drift, can result in a fund that may run counter to your investment goals. The drift may be sudden—say if a new manager comes on board—or it may be more gradual, as the fund shifts its strategy to adapt to changing market conditions. This doesn't necessarily mean you should dump the fund. Change can be good. But you should always know what course your fund is headed on, and have the opportunity to put your money elsewhere if you don't agree with the direction.

Don't assume that the fund's name will always accurately reflect its portfolio. IBM has found its way into quite a few small cap funds, and even the most conservative fund may bet on a tech upstart. Only careful attention can ensure a fund's strategy matches your own.

Mutual Fund Company	Phone Number	Website	Load/No Load?
American Century	800 345-2021	www.americancentury.com	Both
Franklin Templeton Investments	800 632-2301	www.franklintempleton.com	Both
Janus	800 525-3713	www.janus.com	No-load
JP Morgan Funds	800 348-4782	www.jpmorganfunds.com	Both
Oakmark	800 625-6275	www.oakmark.com	No-load
Charles Schwab	877 488-6762	www.schwab.com	Both
Scudder Investments	800 621-1048	www.scudder.com	Both
Strong Funds	800 359-3379	www.estrong.com	Both
T. Rowe Price	800 225-5132	www.troweprice.com	No-load
USAA	800 531-8448	www.usaa.com	Both
Vanguard	800 662-2739	www.vanguard.com	No-load
Wells Fargo Funds	800 222-8222	www.wellsfargofunds.com	Load

Fearless Factor

- *Mutual funds offer a more diversified investment strategy than individual stock picking.* With over 13,000 mutual funds available, you can easily find funds that meet your investment goals.

- *When choosing a fund, be on the lookout for excessive expenses that can eat into your returns.* Loads, high operating expenses, and 12b-1 fees can significantly lower your return rate. Read the prospectus carefully.

- *Most thirtysomethings should reinvest profits from mutual funds.* Unless you urgently need the cash, it's generally a smart idea to plow your returns back into the funds. That money should be used to fund your future—not the iPod you've been craving.

- *Money market funds are safe investments that pay better than checking and savings accounts.* Though yields fluctuate over time, they almost always beat the interest paid on checking and savings accounts. If you don't want to tie your money up in a long-term investment, consider a money market fund.

- *The strategy of a mutual fund can change over time.* If it consistently underperforms or evolves in a direction that doesn't suit your investment needs, consider moving your money into another fund.

9

Keeping the Golden Years Golden: Starting a Retirement Fund

If you think it's hard making ends meet on that paycheck you take home now, think about maintaining that lifestyle when your paycheck drops to . . . $0. No, I'm not talking about losing your job. Unemployment is temporary and you can always collect benefits. I'm talking about what happens when you turn 65 and your working days are behind you. Experts say most people need about three-quarters of their pre-retirement income to maintain the standard of living they're accustomed to. Anything less and you're looking at some downwardly mobile senior years.

In some respects, our grandparents were right—things really were simpler back then. They may not have had digital television or KaZaA, but at least retirement planning was largely taken care of for them. What pensions didn't cover, social security could be counted on to cover for the shortfall. These days, do you know anyone with a pension? And Social Security—don't get me started. Unless you haven't read a newspaper in 15 years, you know that the social security program is in deep, deep doo-doo.

Imagine a retirement plan where you faithfully contribute up to 7.65 percent of your paycheck over your entire working life. Over 40 or 50 years, you've accumulated quite a stash. You retire, you start condo shopping in Florida, and the money's *gone*. That's the reality this generation faces. As things stand now, unless Washington gets serious about overhauling social security, the program will go bankrupt by about 2025. People like you and me stand a good chance of getting zilch. What started as a well-intentioned program to force people to save for their retirement is looking more and more like just another tax.

Adding to the impending crisis is the fact that people live longer than ever before. Not too long ago people retired at 65 and faced an average life expectancy of 70. Five years of living on a fixed income. Big deal. Today, however, the average life expectancy is 75 and climbing. Who knows what it will be in 2029, when today's thirtysomethings begin retiring? 100? With advances in medicine and more of us spending time on the Stairmaster, nothing is impossible.

Responsibility for your retirement rests firmly on your own shoulders. It's a big burden, no doubt about it. Fortunately, you have time on your side. This, as you will soon discover, is your greatest ally. If you're in your early thirties and haven't saved a dime for the Viagra years, don't panic—but don't waste any more time either. Most of us would prefer a future free of government cheese and asking our grown children for handouts. Procrastination is fine for dieting and term papers, but not okay when it comes to your future. The stakes are simply too high. If you haven't given a thought to life beyond the 9-to-5 grind, you're in good company, but it's time to get off your butt and start. All those games of Bingo don't pay for themselves, you know.

Compound This

If you've ever struggled to pay off your credit cards, then you know all about the dark side of interest rates. Each month you dutifully make a payment, but those unforgiving interest rates bring your balance right back up again. Anyone who's battled credit card debt probably flinches just hearing the word "interest." But you don't always have to be on the wrong side of interest rates. In fact you can make interest work for you in all sorts of spectacular ways. When the money earning interest is yours *and* you don't touch it for years, interest rates can be a powerful ally. The reason is compound interest, and it's a critical concept to understand for smart retirement planning. It's so impressive, Einstein called it the eighth wonder of the world.

With compound interest, your interest piggybacks on top of other interest. Provided you don't touch the principal, your ever-growing stash will only continue to generate greater amounts of interest as the years go by. This may not make much of a difference for the first few years of a retirement account, but over time it can, not to mince words or anything, make you stinkin' rich. Check out these figures, which sound almost too good to be true:

- If you start saving $100 a week ($5,200 a year) in a tax-deferred account at the age of 30, with a hypothetical 7 percent interest compounded annually, you would have over $1,194,000 when you turn 70.
- If you saved $200 a week at the age of 30 in the same account, you would have over $2,388,000 when you turn 70.
- If you saved $300 a week at the age of 30, when you turn 65 you would have over $3,582,000!

In these examples, when you start makes all the difference. Look what happens to those totals when you blow through your thirties:

- At 40, $100 a week will earn you about $567,000 by 70.
- At 40, $200 a week will earn you about $1,135,000.
- At 40, $300 a week will earn you about $1,703,000.

When it comes to retirement savings, 40 is definitely not the new 30!

The most important thing to remember is, the earlier you get started, the better. Pick up any other personal finance book and you'll see tons of figures and charts that plot your retirement bonanza if you start planning at the tender young age of 25. To which I have to ask, have all these other financial advisers ever been 25? Twenty-five-year-olds are stupid! They can't see beyond next Saturday night, much less the age of 65. In a perfect world, yes, we would start saving early. But in a perfect world, movie theater popcorn wouldn't have the fat content of six Big Macs and Celine Dion would never have learned English. But this is the world we live in and we have to make the best of it.

Retirement plans such as 401(k) plans and IRAs, the two most popular plans around, give everyone the opportunity to cash in on the rewards of compound interest. Anxiety and guilt won't pay for all those Cadillac Sevilles and snazzy sweatsuits. You're older and wiser now, and hopefully you've notched a few nice raises on your belt. With a little bit of discipline and a firm commitment to start today, there's no reason you too can't reap the benefits of compound interest.

The Tax Man Waiteth

Compound interest alone should be a good enough reason to start a retirement plan, but 401(k) plans and IRAs also offer enormous tax advantages that, short of pulling a Leona Helmsley, you would be hard-pressed to replicate elsewhere. When you invest money in one of these retirement accounts, your money grows untouched by the IRS. With most investments, you pay high capital gains taxes on any returns you make. After you pay these taxes, you have less to invest. With a 401(k) plan or an IRA, all taxes are deferred until you start withdrawing the money after you retire. You'll pay taxes then (the IRS isn't *that* generous), but the actual amount taxed is so much greater that you will still come out far ahead of where you'd be had you paid taxes all those years. Some retirement plans offer additional tax advantages we'll look at later. For now, just know that *when* you pay taxes on a retirement fund can ultimately be more important than how much you put into it. The chart below shows the difference of $10,000 invested in a tax-deferred account verses $10,000 invested in a taxed account:

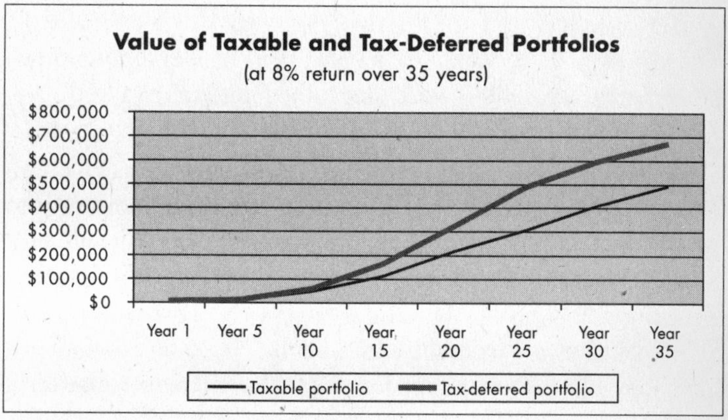

A Very Special K: Welcome to Your 401(k)

Mood rings, designer jeans, and Jimmy Carter weren't the only thing swept away at the end of the '70s. Until then, *pensions* were the retirement plan of choice for millions of Americans. If you're under 40, you probably have only the vaguest idea of what a pension even is. Today, pensions have largely gone the way of the Pinto, replaced by the vastly superior 401(k) and IRA savings plans. The only problem is, both plans are entirely voluntary and many people fail to take advantage of them.

401(k) and IRA plans offer an almost unparalleled investment opportunity for working people. Whereas your grandfather was tied to the same company for decades if he wanted to receive his full pension, 401(k) plans place no such restrictions on job mobility. You can move from firm to firm, and no one can touch your personal contribution. That's a big plus in these job-hopping times. Also, once you set up a 401(k) plan, you're done. The money is deducted directly from your paycheck, so you don't have to worry about your complete lack of self-discipline. (You know who you are.) Soon after the deductions begin, most people don't even notice the difference in their paychecks.

Here's how the typical 401(k) plan works: after a certain period of time (usually a year, depending on company policy), you, the loyal employee, will be invited by your employer to participate in the company's plan. *Take it!* Take it for all of the above reasons, and more. The money you invest in a 401(k) plan is not only tax-deferred but also pre-tax. You already know the advantages of a tax-deferred investing. With pre-tax investing, money earmarked for a 401(k) plan is deducted from your salary *before* federal taxes. This is almost as good as being handed free money and *soooo* much better than investing money that's already been through the IRS wringer. It's like money on steroids. Here's why:

When you contribute to a 401(k) plan, the amount you invest lowers your taxable income. If you made $50,000 last year and contributed $5,000 into your 401(k) account, come tax time, you'd only have to pay taxes on the $45,000. That's even before you start deducting for things like therapy and your "home office." That's a significant tax break the government gives you, just for doing the right thing!

NAVIGATING THE 401(K) JUNGLE

Before the recent market tumble, many workers erroneously viewed their 401(k) plans as turbo-charged savings accounts, secure investment vehicles that year after year miraculously deliver stellar, fail-safe returns. Many of these same people now pour themselves a stiff one before opening their statement, or toss their statements into the trash, unopened and unread. Certainly, the past few years have not been a boon time for investors. But 401(k) plans still offer a solid long-term investment opportunity, particularly for young people who can ride out the bad times. The real danger with 401(k) plans is not the design of the plan, but the choices people make within it. To borrow from my least favorite lobbying organization, 401(k) plans don't kill retirement goals, people do.

Once you become eligible to invest in your company's 401(k) plan (non-profit employers such as schools and charities offer 403(b) plans, which are essentially the same thing), you must decide not only how much you want deducted from your paycheck but where you want to put it. 401(k)s are not one-size-fits-all—they offer a range of choices both in types of investments and degree of risk. Stocks, bonds, foreign, global—you have the same array of choices as when you buy a mutual fund directly.

Where many people go wrong is in how they allocate their money. According to one recent survey, the average worker has over 40 percent of his 401(k) money invested in his own company's stock. *One* stock. That's just crazy. (Many companies will match their worker's contribution with stock, so it's easy to see how an unattended 401(k) can quickly grow lopsided.) Most financial planners recommend investing no more than 10 percent in company stock. Any more and you are essentially speculating with your retirement savings. Not a good move. For an idea of how you should allocate your 401(k) assets, see the breakdowns by age recommended by one leading employee-benefits consulting firm.

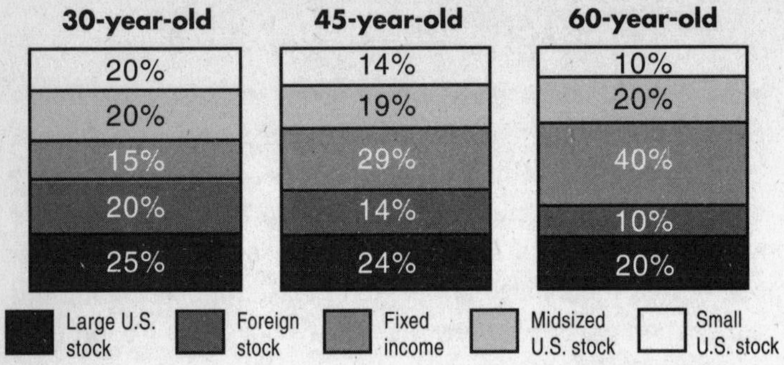

Know Your Limits

Before you get too stoked on the bounty that 401(k) plans offer, know that there are strict limits to how much you can invest. For 2003, an employee could contribute up to a maximum of $12,000 per year. For the next three years, that limit will increase by $1,000 for each year. Depending on your situation, however, that number may be lower. The amount your company matches will affect what you can contribute, and all companies by law impose a ceiling on the percentage of your salary you can invest. So if you've somehow convinced Mommy and Daddy to continue paying all your expenses, you still can't plow your entire paycheck into your 401(k) plan. Instead, try using the extra money to get a life.

The Bad News: 401(k)s Come with Restrictions The Good News: Who Cares!

Many young people open their 401(k) benefits package, get to the part about not being able to withdraw funds without severe penalties until they turn 59½, and read no further. They think, "I'm young. How do I know I won't need that money down the road? I may want to start a business. I may get sick. I want to make money *now*, dammit! Not wait until I'm old and

Not every 401(k) story has a happy ending. Monica, 37, thought she was doing the responsible thing when she opened a 401(k) plan five years ago. She calculates she contributed over $20,000 to it. Today, after five years of disciplined savings, her retirement account is worth . . . $16,000. It's probably safe to say that this is not the direction she had hoped to be going.

It's important to remember that 401(k) plans carry risks, just as any other investment vehicle does. You should never rely solely on your 401(k) plan to fund your retirement. Monica still has plenty of years to recoup her losses and pull ahead, but she's found the whole experience unsettling. "I know retirement is decades away, but I'm a little spooked by this. Thank God I have a house and some other investments so I can sleep at night."

can't enjoy it." To which I say, get real! The percentage you are investing is quite modest. You can certainly find room in your paycheck to pay for all of the other things you want out of life and still save for more immediate goals. Consider dropping your morning Venti Latte habit. You'll save $70 a month. Spend $1.50 on the metro instead of $12 on cab fare. Drop Showtime—the shows suck anway. All these little economies will have only the most marginal impact on your daily existence.

This may be hard to accept, but the government imposes restrictions on your 401(k) plan for your own good. Really! Think about all those things you crave, but put off because you're short the cash. Hawaiian vacation? BMW Mini Cooper? Lipo? In the pursuit of immediate gratification, few of us could resist raiding that growing 401(k) stash. Some of us need a little discipline, and the government is happy to provide it.

There's a good chance your employer will give you some wiggle room, anyway. Many companies will allow you to borrow from your 401(k). The interest you pay goes right back into your account, so this can be a much smarter move than borrowing from a bank. You can also have the repayment deducted directly from your paycheck, which means no worries about late payments. Rules for borrowing vary by employer, so check with your human resources department for specifics.

IRA: The 401(k)'s Little Brother

If these last few pages haven't convinced you that 401(k) plans are the closest many investors will ever get to Heaven, then I haven't done my job well. Either that, or you've been drinking. Regardless of whether it's my explanation or your sobriety at fault, 401(k)s do have one major, unarguable drawback—they're not available to everyone. Worse, who benefits and who gets shafted is based solely on the good graces of your employer. You can't get promoted into a 401(k), and merit won't count much for changing company policy. Last year, the company I worked for produced one of the highest grossing movies of all time. It earned over $800 million in international box office. Everyone was ecstatic, the sequel's already in production, and I still don't have a 401(k) plan.

Individual retirement accounts (or IRAs) offer partial consolation for those denied a 401(k). While admittedly they lack many of the advantages of their 401(k) counterparts, the principle is still the same: you stow money away into a tax-deferred account, and you don't go near it until you turn 59 ½. As long as you have earned income (or are married to someone who has) and are not covered by a pension plan, you can open an IRA. IRAs have nothing to do with your employer. They are offered by institutions such as banks and mutual fund companies. One nice advantage IRAs have over 401(k) plans is you don't have to work a year for a company before opening one. It's a small advantage, perhaps, but it's something.

Before we go into the various types of IRAs available to you,

you should know the most important differences between 401k and IRAs:

- **IRAs don't offer vesting.** Possibly the biggest bummer for those who can't open a 401(k) plan. With a 401(k), if your employer matches your contribution 1:2, and you work at the company long enough to be fully vested, you've earned an automatic 50 percent return. Not even beachfront property in the Hamptons gets you that kind of return! Because IRAs are not an employee benefit, the only money that grows in an IRA is your own.

- **IRAs have lower maximum contribution limits.** For the year 2003, if you are single you can contribute no more than $3,000 a year into an IRA. Of course, you can open as many IRAs as you want, but the total cannot exceed the maximum allowable contribution. (If you are over 50 the limits are slightly higher.) Compare that to the $12,000 your neighbor can sock away into her 401(k) and you begin to see that her plan is Moet to your Michelob. As with 401(k)s, the limits set for future years do take inflation into account, but the lower limits of an IRA will greatly impact the total you'll be able to save.

- **You lose some tax benefits with an IRA.** For single people without access to a 401(k) plan, the government shows some mercy. You can deduct the full amount of your IRA contribution, regardless of your income. If you do participate in a 401(k) plan, you can still open an IRA, but the IRS puts you in a less tax-friendly category. If your adjusted gross income (or a.g.i.) falls below a certain figure, you cannot take your IRA contribution as a deduction. For 2003, single people with an a.g.i. under $40,000 can take the full deduction ($60,000 for couples who file jointly). Those with an annual gross income between $40,000 and

$49,999 ($60,000 and $69,999 for joint filers) are eligible for a partial deduction.

Now, perhaps living in the land of the $500,000 studio apartment has skewed my reality, but these numbers don't exactly seem designed to encourage people to maximize their retirement egg. It is important to bear in mind, however, that tax-*deferred* is still better than taxed-up-the-wazoo. Once the money is in the IRA, it grows tax-free until you start withdrawing the money.

The IRA Grab Bag

Who hasn't experienced the paralysis that can overtake us when asked to make difficult financial choices? If you've ever gone to a restaurant with a 12-page menu and ordered the burger, you know what I mean. It's hard enough committing to a retirement plan when we're staring at 40 more years of work ahead of us. Determining which of the 11 (yup, 11) different types of IRAs is right for you could frighten anyone into putting it off . . . again. Unless your own individual situation is unusual, one of the following types of IRAs will most likely suit your needs just fine.

The Traditional IRA

This is the IRA described above. It is available to all workers, although the tax breaks are better for people without access to 401(k) plans. You can open an IRA at most banks, but it is probably a better idea to go with one of the mutual fund companies mentioned in the last chapter. (Vanguard, American Century, Fidelity, etc.) Banks will often offer fewer investment options for the money you save in the IRA, which can lower your average annualized return. Remember what you learned about the power of compound interest? Over the long haul, lower returns can have very serious consequences on your savings.

As with mutual funds, you should look for a no-load fund with reasonable expense ratios. They're out there, so don't give up after one or two phone calls. You should also speak to an adviser about choosing a fund that takes full advantage of the tax benefits of an IRA. For example, it probably doesn't make sense to join a fund that invests heavily in certain tax-exempt government bonds. Since the interest on these bonds is tax-free anyway, you aren't using your IRA to fully minimize your tax burden. Better to buy tax-exempt investments outside of a retirement account, and use your IRA to shield as much taxable income as possible.

The Roth IRA

If you are single with an income over $110,000 ($150,000 if you're married and file jointly), do yourself a favor and skip this section. This relatively new variation of a traditional IRA is a vast improvement over its older sibling, but it is available mostly to those still in the five-figure club.

With a Roth, you do not get the initial tax deduction, so the money you contribute is after-tax income. However, once the money is inside the IRA, not only does it grow tax-free, but you don't have to pay taxes on it when you withdraw it. That's huge. As long as you keep the money in the IRA for five years, you get the whole pile. The IRS walks away empty-handed.

Roths also come with an additional perk you probably can't appreciate now, but will when you're picking out Christmas gifts for the grandchildren. When you hit 70½, you can keep the money in a Roth IRA, and you keep all of the tax benefits you always had. With a traditional IRA, you are required to pull the money out and put it somewhere else, where most likely you will not enjoy the same tax advantages.

Tim's Story

Tim is a 35-year-old executive in a notoriously volatile industry. Every two years or so he switches jobs. Sometimes he is out of work for several months at a time. Consequently, his income fluctuates wildly. "One year I made $120,000, the next $75,000. It's a wild ride." Tim wanted to maximize his retirement savings with a Roth IRA, but was worried that his high earning years would disqualify him. His solution? He opened *both* a traditional and a Roth IRA. "When I make too much for the Roth, I just put the money into the regular IRA. When I have a bad year, I can contribute to the Roth." For convenience, Tim opened both IRAs with one company. "It's easier that way," he says. "One phone number, one website." Tim's only regret is that he can't double his contribution. "I'm held to the same $3,000 maximum as somebody with only one account. Too bad, because if I wasn't, I'd open three more."

SEP-IRAs

SEP-IRAs allow self-employed people to get in on the retirement savings game. If you work for a company that doesn't offer a 401(k) plan now, there's a pretty good chance that somewhere down the road, you will. Self-employed people won't, however, so SEP-IRAs (or Simplified Employee Pension Individual Retirement Account) give the do-it-yourselfers a chance to maximize retirement investments. With a SEP-IRA, you get to contribute the lesser of 25 percent of your income or $40,000. Now, I know a lot of freelancers who would kill to make $40,000 a year, much less be able to save every penny of it. SEP-IRAs are also designed for small business owners regardless of how high their annual income is. (Note that if you have employees, you may have to contribute for them as well.) SEP-IRAs require more paperwork to set up

Like Mother, Like Son

Some people learn from the mistakes of those who have gone before them. Others have to be beaten over the head before they change. Stephen started his career as an editorial assistant at a lifestyle magazine. Although he didn't make much, he still managed to stash a little cash into his parent company's 401(k) plan. Unfortunately, he also developed some Anna Wintour-sized spending habits. When he left the magazine to pursue a freelance writing career, he couldn't pay his credit card bills and was forced to liquidate his 401(k) plan.

Now a wildly successful self-employed writer, Stephen found ways to spend his ample income on everything but retirement. His girlfriend June stood quietly on the sidelines until one day she finally slammed her foot down. The breaking point came when Stephen's parents decided to split up, and it came out that his parents, though extremely successful lawyers, had very little saved for retirement. "My mother was getting something insane like $30,000 a month from my father during the divorce proceedings, and she complained that she had no money. June heard this and understood exactly where my pathology came from. She insisted that I start saving for my retirement. She found a good financial adviser who helped me open a SEP-IRA. It's hard to believe I was so resistant at first. We almost broke up over it."

Today, Stephen is making up for lost time and contributing the maximum allowable limit to his SEP-IRA. "I don't want to be like my mother," he says. "I love her, but I realize it's hard to garner much sympathy for someone who can't make ends meet on thirty thousand dollars a month."

than a traditional IRA (I set up my plain vanilla IRA online in about 25 minutes), but the savings potential far outweighs the additional headache.

If you already have an IRA and then strike out on your own, you can switch to a SEP-IRA. Call an adviser at your bank or mutual fund company for to learn how to do it. There are many advantages to being self-employed, from the entrepreneurial rush of building something from scratch to never having to answer to chuckleheads. SEP-IRAs offer another great benefit for do-it-yourselfers.

Not Without My 401(k)!

After seven years at the same company, Dylan needed a change. His job in corporate PR was growing stale, and he was ready for new challenges. It didn't take long for the talented writer to get snapped up by a major advertising agency, and within a few weeks Dylan was comfortably settled into his new surroundings. The substantial savings in his previous employer's 401(k) plan, however, stayed behind, and it made Dylan uncomfortable. "The plan invested heavily in my old company's stock, and the company was facing rocky times. I didn't want my retirement tied to that company's future. I also loathe paperwork, so I wanted to consolidate all of my investments with one financial company."

Dylan contacted his mutual fund company and asked about a 401(k) rollover. An adviser explained his options. He could roll the money into an IRA, cash out, or transfer the money into his new employer's 401(k) plan once he became eligible to enroll. Cashing out would mean substantial tax penalties and would also jeopardize his retirement, so that was out. He considered moving the money into his new employer's 401(k) plan, but after the adviser explained to him that an IRA would give him more investment choices than his old 401(k) plan, he decided against it. He was planning to join his new company's 401(k) plan once he becomes eligible, anyway, so he liked the idea of diversifying. Dylan smartly rolled his 401(k) plan into an IRA and enjoys the same tax benefits he had with his employer-sponsored plan.

If you are changing jobs soon, don't forget about your 401(k) plan. Sometimes it may make sense to leave your money in the old plan, but you may be able to do better elsewhere. (Some employers force you to leave the plan when you leave the company, so you may have to move your money even if you don't want to.) The procedure for initiating a 401(k) rollover is usually fairly straightforward, but the steps vary from company to company. (Make sure you specify to your employer that you want a direct rollover—otherwise, the funds may be distributed to you instead of the new account.) Check with your HR department for your company's policy.

KEOGHs

Keoghs (pronounced key-ohz) are considerably more complicated to set up, but offer a small business owner the opportunity to set up a retirement savings plan for both herself and her employees. There are several different types of Keoghs, each with different rules and contribution limits. Some Keoghs allow you to set up a vesting schedule (see below), which you can't do with a SEP-IRA. If you are interested in starting a Keogh, talk to a financial adviser to learn which one best fits your needs.

VESTING

I've mentioned that, unlike pensions, 401(k)s allow you to change jobs without penalty. Strictly speaking, that is correct. The money you've diligently stashed away continues to grow without penalty. However, if your company matches your contribution, they will often require you to stay in their employ for a number of years before the money becomes fully yours. If you leave your job before the allotted time, you lose all or part of your employer's matching funds. This process is called *vesting*.

You should know your employer's vesting schedule before you contemplate changing jobs. Of course, a job opportunity may just be too damn good to pass up. In that case, it might be worth it to forfeit your employer's contribution. If, however, you are considering an offer for no other reason than that the pay is slightly higher, you may come out ahead by sticking with your current employer until you fully vest.

One type of vesting schedule requires you to stay on for a certain number of years (usually three) before receiving your employer's full matching funds. Once you do, however, you are fully vested. You get to keep your employer's full contribution. This all-or-nothing schedule is called cliff vesting. Note that the number of years required usually refers to your start date, not the day you opened your 401(k) plan. Since most employers require you to work for at least a year before you become eligible to participate, it's important to understand the difference. Check with your HR office to double-check your company's policy.

A more common type of vesting is called *graduated* vesting. With this schedule, you receive a higher percentage of your employer's contribution for each additional year you remain employed with the company. Each year the percentage increases incrementally until it hits 100 percent. Say you work at a company that offers a 401(k) plan after one year of employment. You decide to contribute $5,000 a year. (Ordinarily, that number would likely increase with each raise, but let's keep the numbers simple for this example.) A hypothetical vesting schedule might look like this:

Year	Employee Contribution	Employer Matches at 50%	Total Vested	Percent Vested	Value of Vested Sum	Total
2	$5,000	$2,500	$7,500	20%	$500	$5,500
3	$10,000	$5,000	$15,000	40%	$2,500	$12,500
4	$15,000	$7,500	$22,500	60%	$6,000	$21,000
5	$20,000	$10,000	$30,000	80%	$14,000	$34,000
6	$30,000	$15,000	$45,000	100%	$17,000	$47,000

As you can see, sticking around can really pay off. As an added bonus, your boss will chalk up your loyalty to company spirit. Only you and your 401(k) plan need to know the truth.

Fearless Factor

- *Compound interest was made for the young.* Your money grows exponentially the longer you save it. The earlier you start the more you'll have come retirement.
- *IRAs and 401(k) plans offer unsurpassed tax benefits.* You get two nice tax breaks when you open one of these retirement plans: a tax-deductible contribution and money that grows tax-deferred until you withdraw it. Take advantage of these benefits by contributing as much as you possibly can.
- *With a 401(k) plan, diversity is key.* Don't load up on your company's stock. Keep company stock to no more than 10 percent of your account's value, no matter how bright your company's prospects seem. Remember Enron?
- *Look beyond the traditional IRA.* There are eleven different types of IRAs, many of which offer superior contribution schedules and tax breaks if you qualify. Self-employed people should consider SEP-IRAs. Middle-income earners should look into opening a Roth IRA.
- *When you roll over, your money won't play dead.* If you leave your job, rolling your 401(k) plan into another retirement vehicle may offer greater investment options. If you're not satisfied with your old plan, don't be put off by the additional legwork. Your retirement is too important.

10

Debt Be Not Proud

If you're still struggling under a mountain of debt, most of the advice in the previous chapters won't amount to a hill of beans. Perhaps I've been overly optimistic in hoping that as thirtysomethings with adult responsibilities—spouse, kids, dog, etc.—we're in control of deficit spending. Of course, as a recovered credit card junkie, I should know better. Sadly, for many people, debt becomes like a shadow they can't lose. It may grow smaller at times, but, no matter how hard they try, they can't run away from it.

Let's be real. One chapter's not going to hand you the magic bullet for defeating debt. What it can do, however, is help you determine if your problem is one of standard-issue budgeting or if you have the symptoms of a spending disorder. If you suspect you fall into the latter category, counseling may be your best option. For everybody else, this chapter suggests a plan to get your financial house in order.

I Can Stop Anytime I Want . . .

If money is the root of all evil, then what is the root of overspending? Easy credit? Low self-esteem? Satan? Ask ten different experts and you'll get ten different answers. Sadly, the answer is of looming importance to a growing segment of the population. Recent studies suggest that between 1 and 5 percent of all people suffer from some form of compulsive spending. And I'm just guessing here, but I would bet that those percentages skew a lot higher among stressed-out thirtysomethings who came of age in the decade that invented conspicuous consumption.

Most times, poor personal finance habits can be chalked up to indifference, denial, or ignorance. We tell ourselves, "I'm young, I can deal with all this boring financial stuff later." Or, if we're truly delusional, we say, "I'll just ignore my situation and it will go away." For those people, a little education or a reality check can go a long way in correcting the problem. But for a small but burdened minority, overspending often indicates a serious dependency, one that many experts now equate with more traditional addictions such as alcoholism or smoking. If you have a serious spending disorder, budgeting and self-imposed restraint won't do you any good. Professional counseling may be the only solution.

Cindy is a reformed compulsive spender. Back in her twenties, she jokingly referred to herself as a shopaholic. Interestingly, she used her lack of income to disguise the true depths of her problem. "I had a series of dumb entry-level jobs, and I was making no money. So it was easy for me to justify being in debt. I told myself that no one could get by with what I was making, so it wasn't my fault. Besides, I figured I would one day be making better money, so I would just pay everything off then. But when I started making more money, things didn't work out that way. I just found more expensive crap to buy. There was *always* something I wanted that I didn't yet have. Eventually, I was making six figures, but I owed $40,000 on my credit cards. The lightbulb went off. I had a problem, and it wasn't my salary."

For Cindy, now 38, professional help was the only alternative. It wasn't easy for this self-described control freak to admit that she needed outside help. "Money was my Achilles heel," she can now admit. "All the job stuff, my personal life—I just step back, examine the problem from different angles and do what needs to be done." She pauses. "But not when it came to money. I truly felt helpless to stop spending. It was almost as if someone else inhabited my body when I went on those binges." Cindy's day of reckoning came when she calculated how much money she had earned from her first job after college to now. "I made over $1,000,000 and had *nothing* to show for it! No savings, no house, no stocks. A million dollars . . . I just started sobbing."

A good therapist helped Cindy trace her problems back to her childhood and her family's attitudes toward money. "We never had enough, and my mother resented my father for it. It burned her up. She was from a well-off family, and she married down. She felt deprived of the life she felt she was meant to have, and that feeling seeped down to my siblings and me. Her anger made a nightmare of the marriage. As a child, the message I received was that material goods made for a happy home. I was so damn miserable doing without, that I assumed that 'doing with' was the key to happiness."

Your own destructive behavior may be rooted in similar feelings of deprivation that Cindy contended with, or it may be tied to something else. Low self-esteem, distraction from a painful emotional life, substitution for feelings of love and approval—there are as many causes for runaway spending as there are Banana Republics. In a culture that oftentimes cherishes money above all else, it makes sense that our relationship to it might sometimes turn troubling. If you feel you can't get a handle on your money despite your best efforts, the problem may run deeper than mere cluelessness. Do yourself a favor and seek help.

Ten Steps to Take If You Think You Have a Money Disorder

Ron Gallen is a Manhattan-based money counselor who treats clients with a wide range of money disorders, from compulsive spending to hoarding. He is also the author of *The Money Trap,* a prescriptive guide for individuals struggling with psychologically rooted money woes. Gallen himself is a recovered compulsive spender. Here are the ten steps he recommends taking if you suspect you have a serious money disorder:

1. Admit that your problem may go deeper than just money.
2. Stop borrowing money and using credit cards. Close the accounts and cut up the cards.
3. Spend money only when you can pay cash. If you have to have that pair of shoes, take the money out of the ATM.
4. Avoid situations that trigger your spending (favorite stores, envy-inducing or wealthier friends).
5. Don't spend to change your mood.
6. Get clear about your situation. Go through all your unopened bills and make an honest list of your assets and debts.
7. Write down everything you spend, and don't forget the small stuff. Every cent counts.
8. Create a spending plan that takes care of your needs, but more modestly. You can still buy yourself flowers and lingerie, just less often. And once you've cut back, the pleasures you do allow yourself should be guilt-free.
9. Develop a repayment plan with your creditors that won't leave you strapped, even if that means paying less than the monthly minimum required. (Credit card companies are more flexible than you might think.)
10. Get professional help.

Waste Management

You know what your #1 weapon in your fight against debt is? Hint: it's not a better job, fancy budgeting software, or an unexpected inheritance from Aunt Trudy. No, the most powerful tool you have in permanently vanquishing money anxiety is small, affordable, and easy to steal from the office. It's a pen—and you need to learn how to use it.

For most people in their thirties, money problems spring from one place—leaky wallets. We piss away our hard-won salaries on crap. We're years away from worrying about our own kid's tuition payments. The student loan is gone. Our medical bills are probably the lowest they'll ever be. So we blow it in other ways. Four-dollar lattes, fancy cell phones with functions we'll never use, overdraft protection that makes it *so* easy to write checks with money we don't have. All temptations your parents never had to contend with, but which you, as a product of the late twentieth century, do.

Identifying the source of your spending leaks is a full 50 percent of the battle. Trust me on this. Once you discover, for example, that you spent $160 on Frappuccinos one August as I did (not hard when it's 95 degrees outside and there's a Starbucks in your lobby), you will move heaven and earth to find cheaper ways to satisfy those pangs of thirst.

For two solid weeks, I want you to carry a pad and pen and record every single expenditure, regardless of how small. Morning bagel? Log it. Sunday *New York Times*? Write it down. Calvin Klein three-pack? Down it goes. Do this reliably and there's no better way to figure out where your money is going.

Below, a sample spending calendar for three days in the life of "Mary Jean," a typical, albeit entirely fictional, thirtysomething:

Mary Jean's calendar illustrates two critical points. Item by item, none of her purchases is going to break the bank. A quick breakfast at the corner deli: $3.50. Cute skirt bought on a lunch break: $55 (plus $8 for a hastily snarfed sandwich). Drinks

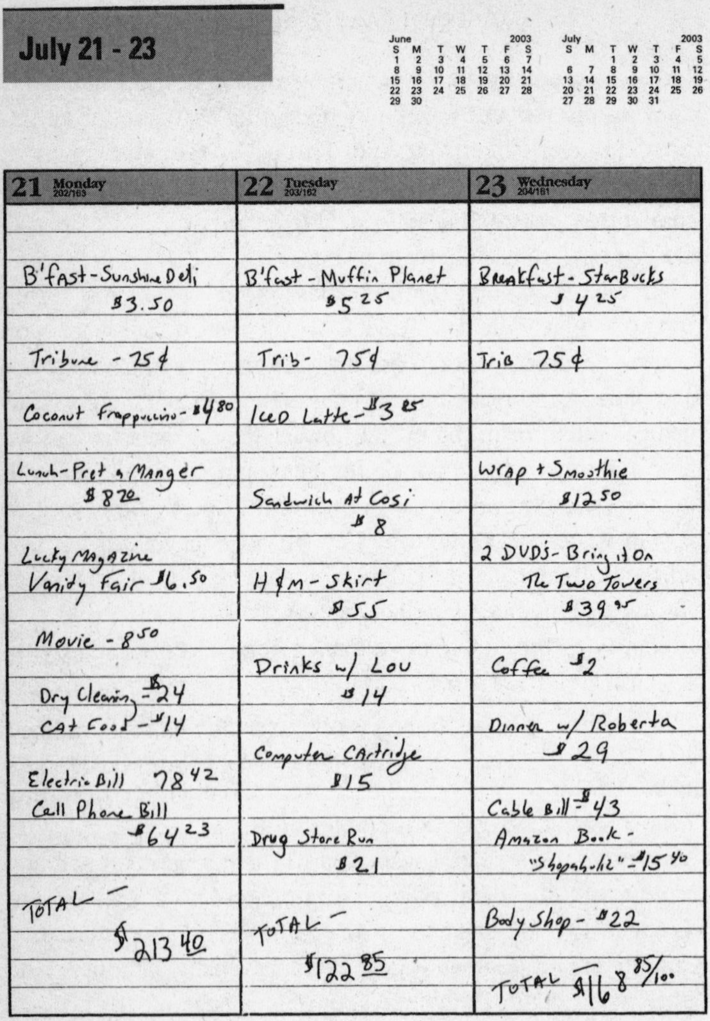
July 21 - 23

June						2003
S	M	T	W	T	F	S
1	2	3	4	5	6	7
8	9	10	11	12	13	14
15	16	17	18	19	20	21
22	23	24	25	26	27	28
29	30					

July						2003
S	M	T	W	T	F	S
		1	2	3	4	5
6	7	8	9	10	11	12
13	14	15	16	17	18	19
20	21	22	23	24	25	26
27	28	29	30	31		

21 Monday 202/163	22 Tuesday 203/162	23 Wednesday 204/161
B'fast - Sunshine Deli $3.50	B'fast - Muffin Planet $5.25	Breakfast - StarBucks $4.25
Tribune - 25¢	Trib - 75¢	Trib 75¢
Coconut Frappuccino - $4.80	Iced Latte - $3.85	
Lunch - Pret a Manger $8.70	Sandwich At Cosi $8	Wrap + Smoothie $12.50
Lucky Magazine Vanity Fair $6.50	H&M - Skirt $55	2 DVD's - Bring it On The Two Towers $39.95
Movie - 8.50	Drinks w/ Lou $14	Coffee $2
Dry Cleaning - $24 Cat Food - $14	Computer Cartridge $15	Dinner w/ Roberta $29
Electric Bill 78.42 Cell Phone Bill $64.23	Drug Store Run $21	Cable Bill - $43 Amazon Book - "Shopaholic" - $15.40
TOTAL - $213.40	TOTAL - $122.85	Body Shop - $22
		TOTAL $168 85/100

after work with co-workers: $22. But just feast your eyes on those end-of-day totals . . . pretty shocking, no? And, though she's "virtual," I bet Mary Jean's calendar resembles that of so many people reading this book. (Maybe you even bumped into her at the H&M!) Hopefully, Mary Jean now understands how everyday living can easily erode a budget.

Now, before you protest that I want to take away everything but your Tivo, chill. Life on an austerity plan is really no life at all. Besides, I have yet to meet anybody willing to go back to P,B & J or spend Saturday nights watching videos borrowed from the local library to get out of debt. And that brings us to our second point:

You Can Do Most of the Same Things for Less

In my office building, there's a Starbucks and a no-name coffee bar. Price of a Starbucks tall American coffee: $1.86. Price at the generic place for the same-size cup: $.92. And guess what? The no-frills coffee tastes *better*! I'm a caffeine addict, and if I don't get my three cups a day it's not fun for anybody. I simply refuse to give up that little indulgence, but by drinking the non-Starbucks brew, I save over $60 a month! For that kind of money, I'll happily forgo the green-and-white Medusa lady on my cup.

Once you complete your own personal calendar, ask yourself what you can and cannot live without. Then, for every activity or item you simply cannot cut, ask yourself if there's a cheaper alternative. I bet there is. Mary Jean, for example, might try eating a piece of fruit in the morning at home. It's cheaper (and healthier) than her daily deli ritual. And that skirt at H&M? Mary already owns three just like it. If she is honest with herself, she might admit that she bought it on impulse, and probably will wear it once or twice before shoving it in the back of the closet. I think you get the point.

Once you start tracking your money, you'll find it relatively painless to reform your profligate ways. With a little determination, you'll soon find yourself hitting the ATM a lot less often and those emergency cash advances will fade to a distant memory. And there's more good news. You've already done the hard part—it only gets easier from here. Admittedly, changing ingrained spending patterns requires considerable discipline and patience. New habits need time to take root and become second nature. The rest of this chapter focuses on quick saving solutions to satisfy your immediate gratification urges. Follow the suggestions here and you'll shave thousands of dollars off the common, unavoidable expenses thirtysomethings face. Some require little more than a phone call. Others may take a little online legwork. But follow the advice here and you'll reap the benefits for years to come.

Is there room for improvement in your spending habits? Take this quiz and find out. (With apologies to *Cosmo*.)

1. Do you know exactly how much you earn but have no idea what you spend it on?____
2. Have you ever lied to someone about how much money you've saved because you know it should be more?____
3. Does your credit card debt always seem to rise with your income?____
4. Does the thought of "doing without" trigger depression or an anxiety attack?____
5. Do you frequently buy clothes you don't wear or gadgets you don't use?____
6. Do you consider buying something on sale as money saved instead of money spent?____
7. Do you sometimes take out cash advances to pay for a vacation?____
8. Do you justify extravagant purchases by scrimping on low-cost, everyday items? (In other words, if you've ever dropped $300 on a sweater and then bought scratchy toilet paper for the rest of the year as penance, that's a "yes".)____
9. Do you claim you can't afford potentially beneficial

things like therapy, yet somehow manage to sustain a $60 weekly latte habit?____

10. Do you often find yourself praying to God that your card isn't declined when you hand it over at the cash register?____
11. Do you find that God only accepts cash?____

Your score:

0–2. Healthy, wealthy, and wise. Everyone's entitled to an occasional slip-up. You have nothing to worry about.

3–5. Flirting with danger. And danger will go home with you and steal your wallet. A little self-restraint . . . please.

6–8. If you ever cancel your American Express card, local merchants will hold a candlelight vigil.

9–11. You would pay for air if it were on sale.

Credit Cards

That guy from *The Graduate* was right. Our future really did belong to plastic! How can one thin little card, weighing less than an ounce, wreak so much destruction? I know many people who've struggled to pay down credit card debt, only to get choked by the balances. More depressing, for all that debt, they have precious little to show. For these people, their self-respect plummets in direct inverse proportion to their skyrocketing debt.

If you're currently struggling with your own credit card troubles, you know the symptoms: self-imposed deadlines that come and go, well-rehearsed pleas to the Visa lady for another credit increase, triple-digit monthly interest charges . . . no wonder you're too exhausted to think about anything else. As someone who by the age of 26 had charged up $15,000 in credit card debt, I know how exhausting carrying around all that anxiety can be. Our brains (well, at least *my* brain) have a finite amount of space to utilize. Who wants to fill it up with this garbage? It becomes impossible to think with a clear head. Resentment creeps in, followed soon after by despair. Why work your ass off to fatten the profits of some devil company in Sioux Falls, South Dakota?

Though it may look pretty grim from the view down there, there is a way out. And, more significantly, you don't have to whittle those balances down to zero before you feel you're once again in control of your life. Empowerment begins the moment you formulate a viable plan. Satisfaction begins when you stick to it. Once firmly established on that repayment track, it's a ride you'll enjoy every step of the way. Below, we probe the enemy—also known as your monthly statement—and unearth his vulnerable spots.

Welcome to Your Monthly Statement

If there's a treasure trove of credit card savings waiting to be discovered, consider your monthly statement your map. Your statement can point the way to "riches" you never dared dream of—slimmed-down interest rates, reduced fees, smarter spending strategies, you name it. Pretty much every square inch of that perforated nightmare is open to attack. If you have your most recent statement, grab it and follow along. If you've already tossed it, fear not—use the statement on the next page as your guide.

A. Annual percentage rate. This is the cash cow for your issuer. With interest rates routinely 20 percent or higher, if you pay only the minimum each month, you will be gumming your meals before you pay off your balance. Think I'm kidding? Take the 36-year-old with the $4,473 balance in the sample statement. If he pays the minimum

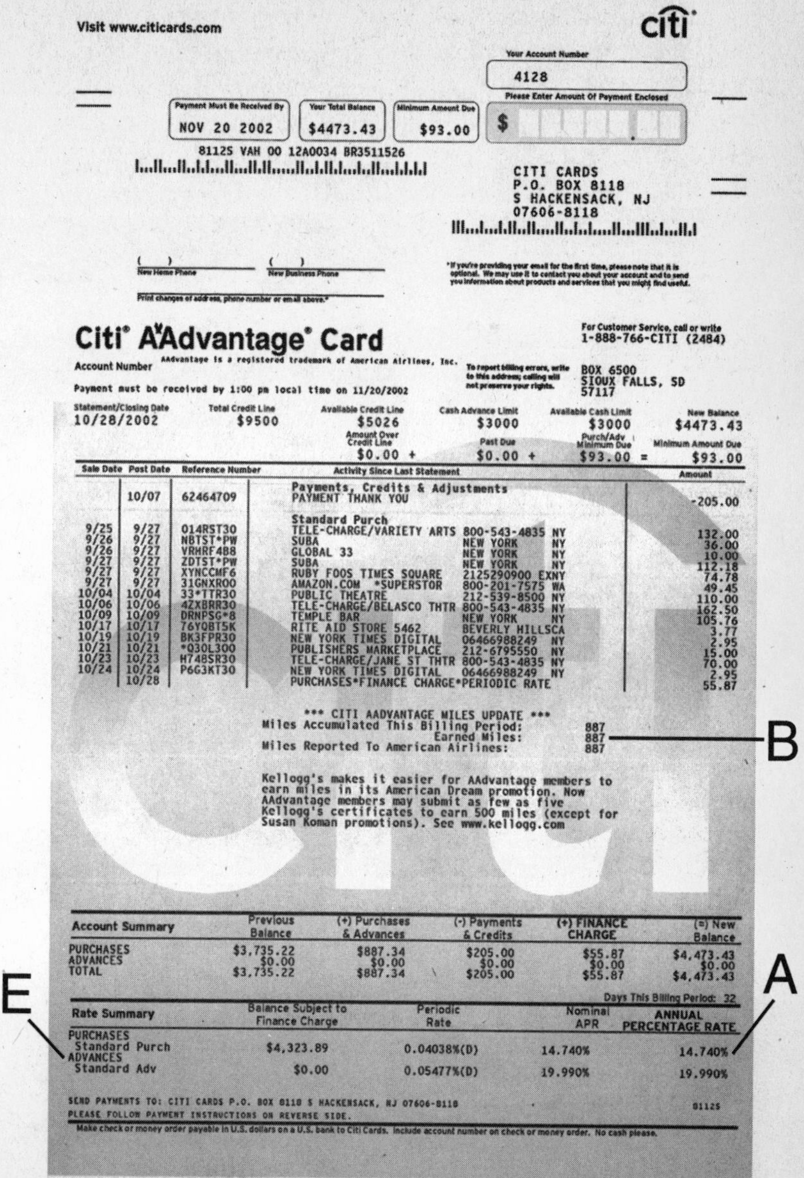

Visit www.citicards.com

Your Account Number: 4128

Payment Must Be Received By	Your Total Balance	Minimum Amount Due
NOV 20 2002	$4473.43	$93.00

Please Enter Amount Of Payment Enclosed: $

81125 VAH 00 12A0034 BR3511526

CITI CARDS
P.O. BOX 8118
S HACKENSACK, NJ
07606-8118

( ) New Home Phone ( ) New Business Phone

Print changes of address, phone number or email above.*

*If you're providing your email for the first time, please note that it is optional. We may use it to contact you about your account and to send you information about products and services that you might find useful.

Citi® AAdvantage® Card

Account Number

AAdvantage is a registered trademark of American Airlines, Inc.

For Customer Service, call or write
1-888-766-CITI (2484)

To report billing errors, write to this address; calling will not preserve your rights.
BOX 6500
SIOUX FALLS, SD
57117

Payment must be received by 1:00 pm local time on 11/20/2002

Statement/Closing Date	Total Credit Line	Available Credit Line	Cash Advance Limit	Available Cash Limit	New Balance
10/28/2002	$9500	$5026	$3000	$3000	$4473.43
		Amount Over Credit Line	Past Due	Purch/Adv Minimum Due	Minimum Amount Due
		$0.00 +	$0.00 +	$93.00 =	$93.00

Sale Date	Post Date	Reference Number	Activity Since Last Statement	Amount
			Payments, Credits & Adjustments	
	10/07	62464709	PAYMENT THANK YOU	-205.00
			Standard Purch	
9/25	9/27	014RST30	TELE-CHARGE/VARIETY ARTS 800-543-4835 NY	132.00
9/26	9/27	NBTST*PW	SUBA NEW YORK NY	36.00
9/26	9/27	VRHRF4B8	GLOBAL 33 NEW YORK NY	10.00
9/27	9/27	ZDTST*PW	SUBA NEW YORK NY	112.18
9/27	9/27	XYNCCMF6	RUBY FOOS TIMES SQUARE 2125290900 EXNY	74.78
9/27	9/27	31GNXR00	AMAZON.COM *SUPERSTOR 800-201-7575 WA	49.45
10/04	10/04	33*TTR30	PUBLIC THEATRE 212-539-8500 NY	110.00
10/06	10/06	4ZXBRR30	TELE-CHARGE/BELASCO THTR 800-543-4835 NY	162.50
10/09	10/09	DRNPSG*8	TEMPLE BAR NEW YORK NY	105.76
10/17	10/17	76YQBT5K	RITE AID STORE 5462 BEVERLY HILLSCA	3.77
10/19	10/19	BK3FPR30	NEW YORK TIMES DIGITAL 06466988249 NY	2.95
10/21	10/21	*Q30L300	PUBLISHERS MARKETPLACE 212-6795550 NY	15.00
10/23	10/23	H748SR30	TELE-CHARGE/JANE ST THTR 800-543-4835 NY	70.00
10/24	10/24	P6G3KT30	NEW YORK TIMES DIGITAL 06466988249 NY	2.95
	10/28		PURCHASES*FINANCE CHARGE*PERIODIC RATE	55.87

*** CITI AADVANTAGE MILES UPDATE ***
Miles Accumulated This Billing Period: 887
Earned Miles: 887
Miles Reported To American Airlines: 887

Kellogg's makes it easier for AAdvantage members to earn miles in its American Dream promotion. Now AAdvantage members may submit as few as five Kellogg's certificates to earn 500 miles (except for Susan Koman promotions). See www.kellogg.com

Account Summary	Previous Balance	(+) Purchases & Advances	(-) Payments & Credits	(+) FINANCE CHARGE	(=) New Balance
PURCHASES	$3,735.22	$887.34	$205.00	$55.87	$4,473.43
ADVANCES	$0.00	$0.00	$0.00	$0.00	$0.00
TOTAL	$3,735.22	$887.34	$205.00	$55.87	$4,473.43

Days This Billing Period: 32

Rate Summary	Balance Subject to Finance Charge	Periodic Rate	Nominal APR	ANNUAL PERCENTAGE RATE
PURCHASES				
Standard Purch	$4,323.89	0.04038%(D)	14.740%	14.740%
ADVANCES				
Standard Adv	$0.00	0.05477%(D)	19.990%	19.990%

SEND PAYMENTS TO: CITI CARDS P.O. BOX 8118 S HACKENSACK, NJ 07606-8118 81125
PLEASE FOLLOW PAYMENT INSTRUCTIONS ON REVERSE SIDE.

Make check or money order payable in U.S. dollars on a U.S. bank to Citi Cards. Include account number on check or money order. No cash please.

Important Instructions for Making Payments

CREDITING PAYMENTS: For payments by regular mail, please allow 5-7 days for your payment to reach us. Your payment must be received in proper form at our processing facility by 1:00 p.m., local time, on a bank business day, in order to be credited to your account as of that day. All payments received at the processing facility in proper form after that hour will be credited as of the following bank business day. There may be a delay of up to 5 days in crediting a payment sent by mail if it is not in the proper form or is addressed to a location other than the address listed on the return envelope or on the front of the payment coupon, or, for courier or express mail payments, to the Express Payment address set forth below. The business days of the bank are Monday through Friday, excluding Federal Holidays.

C

PROPER FORM for payments sent by mail or courier.
For a payment to be in proper form, you should:
- **ENCLOSE** your check or money order. No cash or foreign currency please.
- **INCLUDE** your account number and name on the front of your check or money order.

Additional Instructions
- **DO NOT** staple, tape, or paper clip your check or money order to this payment coupon.
- **ENCLOSE** this payment coupon with your check or money order so that the entire address appears through the window of the envelope that is provided.
- **USE** blue or black ink.

FEES FOR STATEMENT COPIES: On non-disputed matters or any matter unrelated to a billing error, we will charge a $3.00 fee for each duplicate statement that is more than 3 months prior to your request. We will add this fee to your purchase balance.

PAYMENT OPTIONS OTHER THAN REGULAR MAIL:
- The AutoPay system automatically deducts the payment amount you choose from an account you designate. Once your enrollment is effective, your account will be credited each month as of the payment due date.
- Sign up for online payments with Click to Pay at www.registermyaccount.com and follow all the on-screen instructions. If we receive your request to make a Click to Pay payment by 1 p.m. Eastern time on a bank business day, we will credit your payment as of that day. If we receive your request to make a Click to Pay payment after 1 p.m. Eastern time, we will credit your payment on the next bank business day.
- SPEEDPAY by phone. Make your one-time payment quickly by phone using SPEEDPAY (a registered trademark of SPEEDPAY, INC.). You will be charged $9.95 to use this separate payment service. Call by 1:00 p.m. Eastern time, on a bank business day, to have your payment credited as of that day. If you call after that time, your payment will be credited as of the next bank business day.
- Send payment by courier or express mail to the EXPRESS PAYMENTS address: Citibank, Attention: Payment Mail Opening; 111 Sylvan Ave; Englewood Cliffs, NJ 07632. Payment must be received in proper form, at the proper address, by 1:00 p.m. Eastern time, on a bank business day, in order to be credited as of that day. All payments received in proper form, at the proper address, after 1:00 p.m. Eastern time will be credited as of the next bank business day.

REPORT A LOST, STOLEN OR NEVER RECEIVED CARD IMMEDIATELY:
Our Customer Service Representatives are available 24 hours a day, 7 days a week.

Information About Your Account

D

- **ANNUAL MEMBERSHIP FEE:** Refer to your statement in the month in which the fee is billed.
- **RENEWING YOUR ACCOUNT:** You may have your annual membership fee credited to your account if you close your account within 30 days from the mailing or delivery date of the statement containing the fee, even if you use your card during that period. You may call the Customer Service number or write to the Customer Service address on your statement during this 30 day period and your account will be terminated; we will credit your account for the amount of the annual fee.
- **ANNUAL PERCENTAGE RATE:** Refer to the Rate Summary section of this statement. Your periodic rates and APRs may vary.
- **RATE AND ACCOUNT SUMMARIES:** The purchase and advance features of this account may be listed in the Rate Summary Section of this statement under the following titles: Standard Purch, Purch/Adv, Standard Adv, and various numbered Offers. The Account Summary section of this statement includes on the PURCHASES line subtotals for all purchase features, and on the ADVANCES line subtotals for all advance features, of the Previous Balance, new Purchases & Advances, Payments & Credits, FINANCE CHARGE and New Balance amounts.
- **PERIODIC RATES:** (D) and (F) indicate daily periodic rate. (M) indicates a monthly periodic rate.
- **BALANCE SUBJECT TO FINANCE CHARGE – AVERAGE DAILY BALANCE (INCLUDING NEW TRANSACTIONS):** A variety of purchase and cash advance features are available (e.g., Standard Purch, Standard Adv, and various numbered Offers for both purchases and advances). We figure a portion of the finance charge on your account each day by multiplying the daily balance on each feature by the applicable daily periodic rate. We do this each day of the billing period, including the Statement/ Closing Date. To get the daily balance, we take the beginning balance for each feature every day, add any new transactions, fees, and any finance charge on the previous day's balance, subtract any credits or payments credited as of that day, and make other adjustments. A credit balance is treated as a balance of zero. The Balances Subject to Finance Charge are the averages of the respective daily balances during the billing period. If you multiply this figure for each feature by the number of days in the billing period and by the applicable daily periodic rate, the result will be the periodic finance charges assessed for that feature, except for minor variations caused by rounding.
- **SPECIAL CALCULATION METHOD FOR CERTAIN CARDMEMBERS:** If the periodic rate listed in the Rate Summary section of this statement is followed by an "(M)" for Purchases and an "(F)" or an "(M)" for Advances, we use the calculation methods described below to determine the Balance Subject to Finance Charge.
(A) For finance charge calculation purposes, the billing period begins on the Statement/Closing Date of the previous billing period and varies with the number of days in the billing period. To get the Balance Subject to Finance Charge on each feature (e.g. Standard Purch or Standard Adv) we take the beginning balance for that feature every day (including finance charges imposed in previous billing periods), add any new transactions and fees, subtract any credits or payments credited as of that day, and make other adjustments. A credit balance is treated as a balance of zero. This gives us the daily balance. We add up all the daily balances for the billing period (except the balances on the Statement/ Closing Date) and divide by the total number of days in the billing period. This gives us the Balance Subject to Finance Charge for that feature.
(B) We figure a portion of your finance charge on transactions subject to a monthly periodic rate by multiplying the monthly periodic rate by the Balance Subject to Finance Charge (including new transactions). We may figure a portion of your finance charge on advances by multiplying the daily periodic rate, if applicable, by the number of days in the billing period and then applying the result to the Balance Subject to Finance Charge for advances (including new advances).
- **STATEMENT/CLOSING DATE:** At our discretion, this statement may include charges, fees, and payments on the Statement/Closing Date.
- **CHOICE ACCOUNTS:** For CHOICE accounts, cash advances are included in the ADVANCES feature from the day you take them until the Statement/Closing Date of the current billing period. Thereafter, any remaining Standard Adv balance will be included in the Standard Purch feature.
- **GRACE PERIOD FOR REPAYMENT OF BALANCES:**
FOR PURCHASES: If we received payment of the total New Balance, if any, listed on the last billing statement, in the proper form, in time to be credited as of the payment due date on that statement, you have until 1:00 pm local time on the payment due date shown on this statement, which is not less than 20 days, for us to receive, in the proper form, your New Balance to avoid imposition of additional finance charges on purchases. If you have accepted certain balance transfer offers for which you may be eligible, you may not be able to avoid additional finance charges, as described in your balance transfer offer.
FOR ADVANCES: You have no grace period in which to repay your balance for cash advances before a finance charge will be imposed.
- **MINIMUM FINANCE CHARGE:** There will be a minimum finance charge of $.50 for each billing period in which a finance charge, based upon a periodic rate, is payable.

BILLING RIGHTS SUMMARY

- **IN CASE OF ERRORS OR QUESTIONS ABOUT YOUR BILL:** If you think your bill is wrong, or if you need more information about a transaction on your bill, write us at the Customer Service address specified on this statement as soon as possible (you may use, but are not required to use, the 'Notification of Disputed Item' form provided below or a copy of it). We must hear from you no later than 60 days after we send you the first bill on which the error or problem appeared. You can telephone us, but doing so will not preserve your rights.
If you choose to use the form below, please call Customer Service for assistance.
If you send us a letter please include the following information:
  - Your name and account number.
  - The dollar amount of the suspected error.
  - Describe the error and explain, if you can, why you believe there is an error. If you need more information, describe the item you are unsure about.
  - Please be sure all correspondence is signed by the primary cardholder.

You do not have to pay any amount in question while we are investigating, but you are still obligated to pay the parts of your bill that are not in question. While we investigate your question, we cannot report you as delinquent on the disputed item or take any action to collect the amount you question.
- **SPECIAL RULE FOR CREDIT CARD PURCHASES:** If you have a problem with the quality of goods or services that you purchased with a credit card, and you have tried in good faith to correct the problem with the merchant, you may not have to pay the remaining amount due on the goods or services. You have this protection only when the purchase price is more than $50 and the purchase is made in your home state or within 100 miles of your mailing address. (If we own or operate the merchant, or if we mailed you the advertisement for the property or services, all purchases are covered regardless of amount or location of purchase.)

Notification of Disputed Item-Please call Customer Service prior to completing this form.

✂- -

Please sign this form and return it to the Customer Service address on this statement. Do not mail this form with your payment.
If your card has been lost, stolen or you have not received it, call Customer Service immediately. Do not use this form.
Please print in blue or black ink.

CASE ID: ____________________

NAME (PLEASE PRINT) ________________________________

SIGNATURE ____________________ DATE ____________

ACCOUNT # ________________________________

REFERENCE # ____________________ AMOUNT OF DISPUTE ____________

MERCHANT ________________________________

I have examined the charges made to my account and am disputing an item for the following reason:

☐ 1. Neither I nor any person authorized by me to use my card made the charge listed above. In addition, neither I nor anyone authorized by me received the goods and services represented by this transaction. **(If you do not recognize a sale, choose this option and call Customer Service immediately).**

☐ 2. Although I did participate in a transaction with the merchant, I was billed for ________ transaction(s) totaling $________ that I did not engage in, nor did anyone else authorized to use my card. I do have all my cards in my possession. **Enclosed is a copy of the Authorized sales slip.**

☐ 3. I have not received the merchandise that was to have been shipped to me. Expected date of delivery was ________ (mm-dd-yy). I contacted the merchant on ________ (mm-dd-yy) and the merchant's response was ____________________. (In order to assist you, the merchant must be contacted.)

☐ 4. I have (circle one) returned/canceled merchandise on ________ (mm-dd-yy) because ____________________. **Please provide a copy of the return receipt, postal receipt or proof of refund.**

☐ 5. The attached credit slip was listed as a charge on my statement.

☐ 6. I was issued a credit slip for $________ on ________ (mm-dd-yy), which was not shown on my statement. **A copy of my credit slip is enclosed.**

☐ 7. Merchandise that was shipped to me arrived damaged and/or defective on ________ (mm-dd-yy). I returned it on ________ (mm-dd-yy). Merchant response was ____________. **Please provide postal receipt and/or credit slip.**

☐ 8. My account was charged $________, but I should have been billed $________. **Enclosed is a copy of the sales receipt and/or other documents which indicate the correct amount.**

☐ 9. **Other** – Attach letter describing the dispute.

Note: You may write us or use this form (or a copy). However, if you use this form, you may want to record the information on the reverse side for your records.

each month, he'll be 67 years old off and living in a retirement village before he pays it all off.

Many people don't realize that, far from being set in stone, the a.p.r. is actually quite negotiable. How's that? The economics of lending make it possible. It's almost standard operating procedure for young people to rack up several thousand dollars in interest. Faced with losing that kind of easy money, if you're a responsible payer, most banks will negotiate rather than kiss you good-bye.

Call your credit card company and see what they can do for you. Be polite, but firm. Explain that you've been satisfied with the service the bank provides, but you can do better elsewhere. (It's best to have the name of a competitor and their rates handy. Sometimes they ask.) Be prepared for the customer service representative to extol the special benefits their card offers. Listen, and then disregard. You don't need 24-hour customer service or free upgrades at airport Marriots. You need an a.p.r. that doesn't border on the usurious. Chances are you'll get the rate you want. And if not, don't abandon hope. There's always a more reasonable card issuer out there that will be happy to have your business.

B. Miles. Banks dangle tickets and upgrades to their cardholders as incentives to join their so-called "affiliation" programs. Most work the same way. For every dollar you charge, you "earn" a mile toward free travel. On the surface, this sounds like a sweet deal. If you're going to charge stuff anyway, why not get the miles for it? Unfortunately, it's not quite that straightforward. For one thing, affiliation cards almost always charge a higher annual fee than an ordinary card, so you've already paid for a chunk of those miles. And forget about negotiating a lower a.p.r. with an affiliation card. Most will laugh in your face. (I guess they know how many mileage addicts there are out there who will happily pay 21 percent interest just to inch closer to a free ticket to Des Moines.)

The real danger with these cards comes from their power to seduce you into buying crap you just don't need. When you know you're accumulating miles, it becomes easy to justify whipping out the card. And if you're scraping up against a free ticket but not quite there yet—forget it. You've got your "mileage goggles" on. Suddenly even that cubic zirconium junk Joan Rivers hawks on QVC starts looking good.

C. Late fees. Did you know that credit card companies hold you responsible for inclement weather, the pokey U.S. Postal Service, even their own delays in processing your payment? It's true. Every other creditor I can think of—utilities, student loans, the IRS, etc.—considers the postmark on the envelope the date the bill is settled. Most credit card companies do not. They consider the payment date the day they get around to ripping open your envelope and cashing your check. That's why you can mail a payment three days before the due date and still get slapped with a hefty late fee.

Paying online or mailing your payment five to seven business days before the due date is the easiest way to avoid a late fee. However, if you're just an inherently undisciplined person, you can still usually knock those fees off with a phone call. The first time you ask for the fee to be waived, try playing wide-eyed innocent. Practice: "Oh, I thought I just had to mail it by the 17th. I'm so sorry. Can you forgive me just this once? I promise I won't do it again." After that, you'll have to get more creative. Lie. Swear up and down that you sent it in on time. Blame the mail. It's not like the U.S. Postal Service has such an enviable track record. It's easier for the customer service representative to delete it from your account rather than to pick a fight with a valued customer. She probably won't even care—it's not her money, after all.

D. Annual fees. With all due respect, why the hell are you still paying these? I can't open my mailbox without another no-fee, low APR card solicitation falling out. If you feel compelled to waste money, do something more productive with it and send it to me. Unlike your credit card issuer, at least I'll appreciate it.

If the junk mail fairy has somehow skipped your house, you can shop online for better, no-fee deals. Try www.bankrate.com for a list of good cards. Many of these issuers will even arrange electronic balance transfers, so with one click of the mouse, you can eliminate fees from your life forever. (One caveat: check the interest rates of any card before signing on. It doesn't make too much sense saving $50 on an annual fee while racking up interest at 24.9 percent.)

E. Cash advances. You'd get a better deal from Tony Soprano. Just look at those terms in the fine print. No grace period. An a.p.r. several notches higher than the already sky-high rate for purchases. An additional borrowing fee as high as 5 percent. And, most obnoxiously, if you carry a balance, most banks won't allow you to pay off the high interest cash advance first. Most of your payments are applied to the purchase part, whether you want it done that way or not. Yes, cash emergencies happen. Me, I'd rather move back in with my parents than agree to terms like that. This is one offer you should refuse.

D.W.I.: Driving While Indebted

Everyone knows the expression "You are what you drive." And many years ago, before the blizzard of financing and leasing options, this may have been true. Now that anyone with a job and a decent credit rating can tool around in a $40,000 SUV, it's become a little harder to impress your neighbors. But people still seem willing to go broke trying. Look no further than the company parking lot—how many times have you seen some spanking new 3,000-pound behemoth roll into a space, the door swings open, and out pops Goober Dan, the 23-year-old assistant in payroll? Dan's annual take-home is less than the price of the car he drives to work. I don't know about you, but when I see people like Dan, my first thought isn't, "Wow! Nice car!" It's " Wow! What a moron!"

Unfortunately, the temptation to drive a budget-busting car often proves too strong to resist. Many of us can't afford a house yet or any other sizable investment. Thanks to leasing and extended loan programs, a new car is the one big-ticket item we can call our own. Plus, let's be honest. For the male singletons among us, cars can be a convenient shortcut to getting dates. However, once you calculate how much this 8-cylinder aphrodisiac is costing you, spending Friday night with Letterman and a bag of Cheetos suddenly doesn't look so bad.

Your choice of car will impact your wallet for years after you drive it off the lot. Below we discuss the many hidden and not-so-hidden ways a stupid car purchase can ensnare you in a hopeless tangle of expenses. Consider these before you tie the knot with a machine that, sorry to say, *will never love you back.*

Depreciation

Sometimes, of course, taking on additional debt makes good sense. Take mortgages. Even after scraping together a sizable down payment for a house, signing your name to a six-figure loan can be a gut-wrenching experience. Between tax breaks and appreciation, however, real estate is the one investment that will rarely let you down. Or student loans. Graduate school is perhaps the best investment you can make in yourself, one that will pay off in higher future earnings and a more fulfilling career. Unfortunately, after four years of undergraduate tuition, many of us find the parental well has run dry.

The difference between a car and a house or an M.B.A., however, is in what happens after you own them. The latter are investments that will enrich you in some tangible or intangible way. An expensive car, on the other hand, loses money for you by the day. Depending on the model, that loss can be substantial. The chart below gives a sense of how quickly your money can evaporate with each tick of the odometer.

Depreciation Rates of Select Car Models

	Lincoln Navigator	Acura Integra GS	BMW 328ic	Maxima XLS
1998 (new)	$43,300	$20,850	$41,500	$28,128
2000	28,900	16,125	28,900	22,600
2002	22,000	12,800	20,675	14,700

If you lost that kind of money in the stock market, you'd crawl under a rock and hide. Yet because we don't experience the financial loss of depreciation until we put the car up for sale, it's easy to ignore. This doesn't make the loss any less real, of course—it just makes it easier to not beat yourself up for being foolish with your money.

Insurance

It ain't rocket science—fancy cars mean fancy insurance bills. Yet, when deciding how much car they can afford, few people take into account that bi-annual ball-and-chain, also known as the "premium." After the price of the car itself, insurance is the biggest driving expense. Cut your premiums down and you'll realize immediate and significant savings, which will continue to pay off every time you renew your policy.

Need hard numbers? I spent a Saturday afternoon on the phone with insurance companies pretending to shop for a new policy. The first round, I claimed I drove a 2000 Jeep Grand Cherokee. A 2000 Grand Cherokee Limited has a blue book value of about $22,500, so naturally I would have to add comprehensive and collision in addition to liability. State Farm quoted me an annual premium of $4,056, Geico $2,472, and Allstate topped them both with a quote of $4,878. (The joys of driving in New York City . . .) Then I called back, lowered my voice, and asked for quotes for a 1997 Saturn SL. With a book value of $5,500, I could safely do without collision.

Sure enough, the price difference for the two cars proved huge. State Farm offered me a policy for $2,922 (a savings of $1,134), Allstate $3,726 ($1,152), and Geico $1,380 ($1,092). I don't know about you, but I'm a pretty good driver. I want to be rewarded with reasonable rates. When you drive an impractical car, regardless of your driving record, you pay through the nose for insurance that is supposed to protect your financial health. Ironic, huh?

Well, Then, I'll Just Lease

Bad idea. To the young and naïve, leasing sounds like a smart move. You get to tool around in a spanking new car, your monthly payment is usually lower than a new car loan, and, provided you don't play interstate Rollerball with it, you just return it to the dealer after three years and get yourself a brand-new ride. Many times you don't even need a down payment. But, like all things that seem too good to be true, leasing is a sucker's game.

If leasing is such a bad idea, why, you might rightly ask, does everybody seem to do it? Well, for one thing, people are like magpies—we like shiny new objects. With its lower monthly payments and no-money-down policies, leasing enables people to drive a new car every couple of years, often one they could otherwise never afford to own. That alone makes the whole shady endeavor worth it to many. Plus, leasing is unarguably convenient. You never have to worry about placing classified ads and haggling over price with strangers when it's time to sell. You simply pull into the dealer's lot, hand over the keys, and walk (or drive) away.

But you have to remember, the guys at the auto companies are not idiots. (OK, maybe the guy who designed the Pontiac Aztec is an idiot, but he's an exception, and probably out of a job.) They wouldn't be so gung-ho about leasing if it didn't fatten their bottom line. Since the payments you make over the life of the lease agreement don't build equity in the vehicle, you are left with nothing at the end of the term. Most leasing contracts are structured so that your total payments more than make up for the depreciation hit, so it is almost always better to own. Tack on acquisition and disposition fees, mileage caps, and other assorted expenses such as gap insurance (basically, extra insurance you carry on top of your primary insurance) and you begin to understand why *"leasing"* rhymes with *"fleecing."*

Credit Worthy

You can't talk about debt without talking about credit reports. With so much riding on good credit, you should commit to checking it once a year for errors. The big three credit reporting agencies are notorious for making mistakes. Federal legislation has made it a lot easier to correct errors than it used to be, although we've all heard the horror stories of innocent people trying to clear up a $40 error and getting caught in a Kafkaesque bureaucratic nightmare.

Since all three credit reporting agencies operate independently, you'll need to check out what each is saying about you. A mistake might appear on one, two, three, or none at all. You can't know unless you read all three. Reports can be ordered from the following:

Equifax, P.O. Box 740241, Atlanta, GA 30374; (800) 685-1111; equifax.com

Experian, P.O Box 2104, Allen TX 75013; (888) 397-3742; experian.com

TransUnion, Consumer Disclosure Center, P.O. Box 1000, Chester, PA 19022; (800) 888-4213; transunion.com

There is a small charge—no higher than $10—but this is a pittance compared to what you'll be paying in higher interest rates if you discover a mistake. Also, if you are denied credit, or live in certain states, you are entitled to a copy of your report free of charge.

If you do discover a mistake, fix it. Send a certified letter to the agency explaining why you believe the information on the report is in error. By law, the agency has 60 days to respond. They can notify you with an explanation of why they believe the information is accurate or they must delete the error from your report. If the information is not removed, but it looks like you will have a hard time winning your case, you can submit a brief (100 words or less) letter explaining your side of the dispute. This letter becomes a part of your record and by law must be sent to any institution that requests a copy of your report. Don't get pissy. A concise, professional explanation will get you further with a lender than one laced with a string of Tourette-like obscenities.

Incidentally, if you're thinking of hiring one of those companies that promises to repair your credit, don't. They are useless at best, fraudulent at worst. Whatever the guy on the phone promises, they don't know any legal loopholes or have a well-placed friend who can delete accurate bad news from your report. The money you pay to them would be better spent going toward settling those debts they're promising to erase.

Credit Repair

There are two kinds of debtors in this world: those who pay their monthly bills on time and those who stuff them in the drawer, turn on *American Idol*, and hope they're gone in the morning. (These are probably the same people who, as kids, ignored Spot's little "gift" at the foot of the stairs, stepping over it for *days* instead of just cleaning it up.) On-time bill payers, no matter how much debt they carry, are rewarded with pristine credit ratings. Those who treat deadlines more, shall we say . . . *flexibly,* get hammered by the credit agencies. This is why two people who carry the exact same amount of debt can have dramatically different credit ratings. It's all in the timing. (Your credit *score*, which creditors are growing increasingly dependent upon, does consider the amount of debt you carry. We'll talk about that in a minute.)

If you've survived this long in the world, I don't have to tell you why a good credit rating is important. Everyone from your landlord to a bank to a prospective employer can access it. If what he sees suggests a checkered past, such information can, and often will, be used against you. Over the years the major credit reporting agencies have grown increasingly sophisticated at collecting every piece of minutia related to your financial life, so it's virtually impossible to hide past mistakes you'd like to put behind you.

Credit Scores

Think of a credit report as your homework and the credit score your grade. Your credit report contains a stunning amount of information, from every address you've ever lived at to names of past employers to the last time you were late with that student loan payment. What it does not do is try to predict your risk as a borrower. That's where the credit score comes in.

The widely used FICO score (developed by a company called Fair, Isaac and Co.) takes all of the information on your report, puts it in a blender, and spits out a score that is supposed to predict your reliability as a borrower. While studies have shown that the score is generally an accurate forecast of risk, it does not account for individual circumstances. For example, FICO penalizes people who carry high credit card balances, regardless of payment history. So even though you might never miss a payment, if you carry a balance month-to-month, your credit score will be lower. This happened to me. I sometimes am forced to carry heavy work-related expenses on my credit card while I wait for Justine in Accounts Payable to reimburse me. This obviously has no bearing on my risk as a borrower, yet it lowers my overall credit score. Other factors affecting your credit score include the actual length of your credit history and the number of times you have applied for credit in the past year.

For more information regarding your credit score and tips on how you can raise it, check out www.myfico.com.

What can you do if the damage has already been done? You've reformed your wicked ways, and now you want the whole world (or at least lenders) to know it. The best thing you can do is wait. Only time can completely heal a spotty credit report. Negative information disappears from your report after seven years, personal bankruptcies *(gulp)* after ten. However, this doesn't mean that you will be a cash-paying credit pariah until the year 2013 rolls around. Every time you make a payment on time, it's recorded on your report. Once you establish a history of paying your bills on time, you will probably find a creditor willing to take a chance on you. You may have some explaining to do, and you'll almost certainly get socked with a higher interest rate, but you can take comfort in knowing you are well on your way to joining the creditworthy.

Laid Off, Stressed Out

If you lost your job recently, you probably noticed that you weren't the only one hanging around the Starbucks on Monday afternoons. Considering over 1,000,000 people were laid off in 2002, you probably had just as much trouble finding a seat to enjoy your latte as you used to on the 8:02. The era when companies engaged in bidding wars for college grads is past. There was a time not too long ago when I didn't have a single friend out of work. Now I have many. Worse, many of them naïvely bought into the new economy lunacy of "productivity miracles" and endless growth and didn't prepare for trouble on the horizon. Now, some of these former high-flyers who were living the good life on six figures haven't seen a paycheck in five months.

If you are nervous that your job is on the line, start planning *now* while you still have a job. The stress of being out of work is great enough. Losing a job is often an emotionally overwhelming experience—hardly the best time to worry about vitals such as health insurance and unemployment benefits. Doing the research now will also bring you valuable peace of mind knowing that you'll get by just fine should the ax fall.

Unemployment benefits: Benefits vary state by state. If you live in California and you get pink-slipped, you're eligible to collect up to $370 a week for a full year. Hardly a king's ransom, but a whole lot better than stingy Missouri, with its maximum weekly benefit of $250 per week. Contact your state unemployment-insurance agency for an explanation of benefits.

Don't forget that as income, unemployment is considered taxable by our supremely unsympathetic government. Talk about kicking a man when he's down! The government doesn't take its share out immediately, but you are responsible for the taxes when you file. Don't assume you'll have another job by then to pay them. Set aside the money each week, and forget it's there. It's not your money, as the I.R.S. will sternly remind you come April 15.

Severance: No company is required by law to offer severance. Unless you're a contracted employee and severance terms are spelled out in your contract, you're at the mercy of your company's largesse. Traditionally, severance packages offer two weeks' salary for every year of employment. Senior executives usually receive more, typically a month. Check with your human resources department to find out what your company's policy is. Provided your company is in decent financial shape, they will probably honor established policy.

Safety cushion: Once you know how much you can collect from unemployment and severance, tabulate how much you need to pay your monthly expenses. Include rent, mortgage payments, utilities, credit card minimums, your phone bill—everything. Chances are that severance and that little unemployment check won't cut it. Begin squirreling away money *now* to cover about three months of living expenses. Open a savings account and don't touch it. If you truly feel your job is vulnerable, consider only paying the minimums on your credit cards for a while so you can beef up your safety cushion. If you lose your job, cash on hand will be far more valuable than a lower balance.

Health insurance: Trying to buy an individual or family health insurance policy on your own can easily surpass the total of your unemployment benefits. For most of us, that's simply not an option. Fortunately, the Consolidated Omnibus Budget Reconciliation Act (better known as COBRA) requires most employers to offer laid-off workers health insurance at the company's discounted group rate. Unfortunately, your ex-company stops picking up most of the tab. That means you're stuck with the entire premium, which will cost you around $450 a month. This is a devastating expense when you're out of work.

If you can't swing that, or if your company has gone under and no longer offers insurance, look into short-term health insurance offered by many of the major carriers. They're still not cheap—expect to pay about $300 a month with a steep deductible. However, they're still preferable to catastrophic policies, which I don't recommend. As the name implies, these policies tend to cover only the most devastating injuries and illnesses. They come with such heavy exclusions that several states have outlawed them. So a common flu shot may not be covered, but a concussion incurred while jumping into a pile of cow manure from a moving SUV might be. Perfect for a guy on Jackass, but probably not much good to you.

Fearless Factor

- *Spending beyond your means may indicate a deeper emotional problem.* Sometimes a problem with debt is about more than not making enough or not making a budget and sticking to it. If you struggle with money, the quiz on page 184 may help you decide if you need professional help.
- *To trim your expenses, you first have to know where your money is going.* It's the little things that wreak havoc with our budgets. To learn why your wallet is always empty, write down all your expenses for a couple of weeks. You'll be shocked at what you discover.
- *Beware of sneaky credit card tricks.* Creeping interest rates and ridiculous fees are just two ways credit card issuers squeeze money out of you. Don't take it lying down—negotiate a better deal for yourself, or take your business elsewhere.
- *Don't let your car drive you down the highway to hell.* Cars are a money pit. If you want to save a bundle on driving expenses, buy used, do not lease, and don't drive a gas-guzzling S.U.V.
- *Check your credit rating and credit score every year.* Many lenders and insurers use your credit report to determine the rates they offer you. A lower score may mean higher rates. Check with the credit report agencies regularly to make sure there are no errors on your report.

Conclusion

Whew! Ten chapters later, you (hopefully) understand that mastering your money requires more than just studying the stock tables and scoring the right piece of real estate. A healthy mental outlook and measured self-awareness will help you attain your financial goals faster than a fancy Wall Street salary. I'm sure you can point to someone in your own life who makes piles of money and has little to show for it. In most cases, the roots have more to do with psychology than financial misfortune.

When you don't have your inner life together, no amount of money can protect you from yourself. Look no further than deposed King of Pop and devoted daddy Michael Jackson. Here's a guy who by the age of 30 had raked in—I don't know, a billion dollars?—more than you and I will likely see in a hundred lifetimes. Today, while he's hardly reduced to asking LaToya for handouts, he's worth a mere fraction of what he was once worth. All those llama farms, epi-facials, and multimillion-dollar legal settlements take their toll. There are two invaluable lessons in Jackson's story: A) no one is immune from financial mismanagement and B) when you try to look like Diana Ross, your nose might fall off.

Over the course of this book, I spoke to dozens of people about their dysfunctional relationships with money. Many spoke to me eagerly, and told me afterward that they found the experience surprisingly cathartic. Others were understandably more reluctant. Opening up to a complete stranger requires exploring painful issues sometimes buried in the deepest parts of the mind. These people came away from our sessions exhausted and frequently upset. I believe, however, that they took an important first step to achieving financial health.

When Tanya, my agent, read an early draft of my manuscript, she pointed out that there was a double standard at work here. She rightly noted that though I had taken pains to assure participants that there was no shame in admitting to financial troubles, there was very little of my own story in the book. I was hiding behind my role as interrogator. Tanya, who is also a good friend and knows me about as well as anybody, called me on it. She reminded me that it is hypocritical to tell people one thing and live by another.

So this is where I get personal.

I can speak so confidently about the intersection of psychology and finance because for most of my life I stood at its crossroads. My financial life didn't stand a chance against my unresolved emotional issues and raging resentment. Only after much therapy-mandated introspection was I eventually able to come to terms with the roots of my debilitating anger and destructive impulses.

In the house I grew up in, money wasn't used to improve the lives of family members. Instead, it was an inescapable source of fear and anxiety. We were raised to believe that we were always just a few bills away from financial collapse. In the face of impending catastrophe, any material wish, no matter how normal, was met with a stony denial. How could we be so selfish when the family was on the brink of losing it all?

But even in my young, unformed mind, this didn't compute. We lived in a suburb teeming with doctors and businessmen. Our town had no shortage of million-dollar homes, and the school district was one of the highest-ranked in the state. Every year my high school sent more than its fair share of graduating seniors to Ivy League schools. In these surroundings, how could we be steps away from the poorhouse?

The answer is, we weren't. Growing up, I didn't yet fully understand how wide the gap between perception and reality can be. My parents were troubled, but, of course, a person can only seek help when she recognizes that there's a problem. Neither did. What most people would consider bizarre and obsessive behavior, they instead chalked up to frugality. Nothing was exempt from their cost-cutting ways. I mean nothing. Even something as mundane as bathing. In the interest of shaving a few dollars off the hot water bill, we were put on a strict, closely monitored schedule of one shower every other day. Sometimes during the dog days of August, if we had played a particularly grueling Little League game, the rules would be relaxed. But usually not.

Few kids have the cognitive sophistication to see this sort of behavior as the mark of a troubled perspective with no rational basis. I was no exception. I interpreted my parents' actions to mean that I was worthless and undeserving. I internalized shame, and carried around horrible feelings of guilt and low self-esteem. Already vulnerable, I never had to look far for another example of how little value I had in my parents' eyes. After my grandmother passed away, my mother inherited a very sizable estate. Though it happened over 17 years ago, to this day I still recall how stunned and hurt I felt when I asked for help with my college tuition. My mother responded, "That money has to last my husband and me the rest of our lives."

I entered my early twenties still dazed from the experience of living in such a bizarre environment. I was now free, but at that point the damage was already done. As an adult, I bristled at any sort of limit imposed on me, especially financial ones. I had such contempt for my parents' values that I couldn't see at the time the benefits of self-restraint and moderation. For me, I equated any restriction with uncomfortable memories of being told we were too poor to afford food and hot water. Armed with a generous credit limit and deferrable student loans, I never denied myself anything.

Sliding deeper and deeper into the hole, I realized that if I didn't address the underlying issues, all of this emotional baggage was going to wreck my future. It took professional help, but eventually I developed a strong enough self-image to tackle my teetering finances. One painful but necessary step required me to distance myself from the familial source of the problem. Only then, after I was on solid psychological ground, was I able to develop a practical plan to dig myself out of trouble.

I did, eventually. As a result I'm now fully able to use my thirties to lay the tracks toward a healthy financial future. If you think you don't have it in you to get over your demons and act your financial age, I say, don't just look at the people in this book. Look at me. I don't make seven figures, I'm not a stock soothsayer, and I didn't marry a millionaire. Through nothing more than commitment and the desire to change, I managed to pull myself back from the financial brink. So don't tell me that you can't too.

Recently, I had an experience that showed me just how far I had come. A relative discovered that my mother had in her possession a substantial number of U.S. savings bonds that my grandmother had left for me. I had known about the bonds since I was in college, but I had written them off. I knew they would never be turned over to me voluntarily, and I didn't think I could handle the psychological pelting I would have to endure to have them returned to me. This relative generously offered to intervene on my behalf. Figuring I had nothing to lose, I gave him my blessing. I'll spare you the details, but suffice it say, all that drama I had left behind came roaring back. Hostile letters were exchanged, excuses made, conditions imposed. Most hurtfully, my mother even tried to claim that many of the bonds in my name that my grandmother bought for me actually belonged to her.

What surprised me was not how venomous the ordeal quickly turned, but how I responded. This time, I didn't blame myself. I didn't use the stress of the situation as an excuse to indulge in self-destructive behavior. I didn't drive myself crazy trying to reason with someone who could not be reasoned with. I took what I had learned in my twenties and stripped all emotion from the situation. I treated it as nothing more loaded than a business transaction. I consulted a lawyer, started a long and protracted negotiation process, and got my bonds back.

They say that time heals all wounds, but I don't believe the saying applies to your internal ones. For those, you'll have to work a little harder than just watching the hands on the clock go by. If you're not where you expected to be financially at this age, the time to address the issues that are holding you back is *now*. Whether your goal is a first home, a worry-free retirement, or a marriage built on mutual financial understanding, the sooner you resolve what's keeping you from these things, the more time you'll have to enjoy them. Life is long and you're still young. Lay the foundation now and you too will look forward to a future that is fulfilling, prosperous—and, yes—fearless.

Enjoy your thirties.

Index

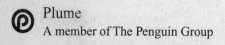